QADIRA ABDUL

RAMADAN TRADITIONS IN IRAQ

A GUIDE TO THE SACRED PATH OF ISLAMIC RITUALS AND PRACTICE IN IRAQ

Contents

INTRODUCTION

BACKGROUND OF RAMADAN IN IRAQ

Ramadan, a sacred month in the Islamic calendar observed by Muslims worldwide, holds a special place in the hearts of the Iraqi people. It is a time of spiritual reflection, community bonding, and cherished cultural traditions. Exploring the background of Ramadan in Iraq allows us to delve into the rich heritage and customs associated with this holy month.

Historical Significance

The practice of fasting during Ramadan has been an integral part of Islamic tradition since the time of Prophet Muhammad. In Iraq, the roots of Ramadan stretch back centuries, with the country being home to a diverse Muslim population, including both Sunni and Shia Muslims.

Cultural Influences

Iraq's unique cultural heritage has left an indelible mark on the way Ramadan is celebrated in the country. The rich history of Mesopotamia, the cradle of civilization, has influenced the customs and traditions observed during this sacred month. Moreover, Iraq's geographical location in the heart of the Middle East has exposed it to various cultural influences from neighboring countries, further enriching its Ramadan traditions.

Religious Observance

Ramadan in Iraq is a time of devout religious observance. Muslims in Iraq fast from dawn to sunset, refraining from food, drink, and other physical needs. The fast is seen as a means of purifying the soul, practicing self-discipline, and empathizing with those less fortunate. It is also a time for increased prayer, recitation of the Quran, and acts of charity.

Social and Community Aspect

Ramadan in Iraq is not only a period of personal reflection but also a time for strengthening community bonds. Families and friends come together to break their fasts, known as iftar, fostering a spirit of unity and togetherness. Sharing meals during iftar nurtures a sense of solidarity and reinforces the importance of family and community in Iraqi society.

Traditional Customs and Practices

Iraqi culture is deeply rooted in traditions, and Ramadan is no exception. The month is marked by various customs and practices that have been passed down through generations. For instance, the firing of cannons or the beating of drums announces the beginning and end of the fast each day, serving as a reminder for Muslims and adding a touch of festivity to the month.

Culinary Delights

Food plays a central role in Ramadan traditions in Iraq. Special dishes are prepared for iftar, often featuring traditional Iraqi flavors and ingredients. From samoon (a type of bread) to dolma (stuffed vegetables) and masgouf (grilled fish), these culinary delights not only satiate hunger but also bring families and communities together to share in the joy of breaking the fast.

Cultural Events and Festivities

Ramadan in Iraq is also marked by a vibrant array of cultural events and festivities. Night markets, known as "souks," come alive during this month, offering a wide range of goods and delectable treats. Traditional music and dance performances, such as "mawal" and "chobi," are organized to celebrate the spirit of Ramadan. These events provide an opportunity for people to gather, enjoy entertainment, and revel in their shared cultural heritage.

The background of Ramadan in Iraq unveils a profound connection between religion, culture, and community. The month of Ramadan holds immense significance for Iraqis, who wholeheartedly embrace its traditions and customs. From the historical and religious aspects to the social gatherings and culinary delights, Ramadan in Iraq is a time of spiritual reflection, communal harmony, and cultural celebration. Understanding the background of Ramadan in Iraq allows us to appreciate the beauty and diversity of this holy month in the country, as it continues to shape the lives and traditions of the Iraqi people.

THE SIGNIFICANCE OF RAMADAN IN IRAQI CULTURE

Ramadan holds a profound significance in Iraqi culture, serving as a time of spiritual introspection, communal solidarity, and charitable acts. Iraqis eagerly anticipate the arrival of this holy month, as it brings a sense of unity and devotion to their faith. In this section, we will delve into the various facets that make Ramadan a cherished and meaningful period within Iraqi culture.

A Time for Spiritual Renewal and Contemplation

Ramadan serves as a period of spiritual renewal and contemplation for Iraqis. It is regarded as a month of heightened spirituality, during which individuals strive to strengthen their connection with Allah and seek forgiveness for their transgressions. Fasting during Ramadan is seen as a means of purifying the soul and deepening one's devotion to Islam. Iraqi Muslims engage in increased prayer, recitation of the Quran, and acts of worship to enhance their relationship with Allah.

Strengthening Bonds of Family and Community

Ramadan fosters the strengthening of familial and communal bonds among Iraqis. The act of fasting and breaking the fast together cultivates a sense of unity and solidarity. Families gather for iftar, the meal that breaks the fast, and partake in the blessings of Ramadan. It is a time for loved ones to reconnect, share stories, and reinforce familial ties. Communities also organize iftar gatherings, where individuals from diverse backgrounds come together to break their fast and nurture a sense of togetherness.

Acts of Charity and Generosity

Charitable acts hold great significance during Ramadan in Iraqi culture. Giving to those in need during this sacred month is believed to bring abundant blessings. Iraqis engage in various acts of charity, such as providing food and essential supplies to the less fortunate, donating to charitable organizations, and supporting community initiatives. Many Iraqis also participate in the tradition of "zakat," which involves giving a portion of their wealth to those in need. This emphasis on charity and generosity during Ramadan reflects the compassionate and caring nature of Iraqi society.

Cultural Traditions and Customs

Ramadan in Iraq is characterized by unique cultural traditions and customs. One such tradition is the firing of cannons or the sounding of drums to announce the end of the fasting day and the beginning of iftar. This age-old practice adds an element of excitement and anticipation to the breaking of the fast. Additionally, homes and streets are adorned with vibrant lights and lanterns, creating a festive ambiance throughout the month. These customs and traditions contribute to the cultural richness and heritage of Iraq.

Preserving Iraqi Heritage

Ramadan plays a vital role in preserving Iraqi heritage and traditions. It is a time when traditional Iraqi dishes and recipes are lovingly prepared and shared among families and communities. Iraqi cuisine during Ramadan is renowned for its tantalizing flavors and unique blend of spices. Delicacies such as "tashreeb," a flavorful soup with bread, and "qima," a spiced ground meat dish, are passed down through generations, serving as a reminder of the rich culinary heritage of Iraq. These culinary traditions not only nourish the body but also celebrate the cultural diversity and heritage of the Iraqi people.

Fostering Unity and Tolerance

Ramadan in Iraqi culture promotes unity and tolerance among individuals of different backgrounds and beliefs. It is a time when Muslims and non-Muslims come together to celebrate the values of compassion, empathy, and understanding. Non-Muslims in Iraq often join their Muslim friends and neighbors for iftar, fostering inclusivity and harmony. This spirit of unity and tolerance during Ramadan reflects the diversity and acceptance deeply ingrained in Iraqi culture.

In conclusion, Ramadan holds immense significance in Iraqi culture. It serves as a time for spiritual reflection, strengthening familial and communal bonds, engaging in acts of charity, preserving cultural traditions, and promoting unity and tolerance. The observance of Ramadan in Iraq is a testament to the profound faith and values that shape Iraqi society.

THE PURPOSE OF THE REPORT

The primary objective of this report is to provide an in-depth exploration of the unique Ramadan traditions observed in Iraq. It aims to offer readers a comprehensive understanding of the cultural significance of Ramadan in Iraqi society and shed light on the diverse customs and practices that shape this holy month. By delving into the preparations, fasting rituals, family and community gatherings, the Night of Power (Laylat al-Qadr), and the joyous celebration of Eid al-Fitr, this report seeks to provide a fresh perspective on the rich tapestry of Iraqi Ramadan traditions.

Through this report, readers will gain valuable insights into the historical and cultural background of Ramadan in Iraq, as well as the religious and spiritual significance it holds for the Iraqi people. By examining various aspects of Ramadan, including the announcement of the month, pre-Ramadan preparations, fasting rituals, and the importance of charitable acts, readers will develop a comprehensive understanding of the customs and practices that define this sacred month in Iraq.

Furthermore, this report aims to highlight the role of family and community gatherings during Ramadan. It will explore the significance of iftar gatherings with loved ones, the vibrant mosque activities, and the community events that foster a sense of unity and togetherness. Additionally, the report will delve into the traditions and customs associated with visiting relatives and neighbors, as well as the special Ramadan traditions cherished by children, emphasizing the importance of fostering strong community bonds and familial connections during this holy month.

Moreover, this report will delve into the significance of the Night of Power (Laylat al-Qadr) in Iraqi culture. It will explore the worship and prayers performed on this auspicious night, as well as the mosque activities and cherished traditions that take place. By understanding the cultural and religious significance of Laylat al-Qadr, readers will gain a deeper appreciation for the spiritual journey undertaken by Iraqi Muslims during Ramadan.

Furthermore, this report will provide insights into the celebration of Eid al-Fitr, the joyous festival that marks the end of Ramadan. It will explore the preparations leading up to Eid, including the special prayers and sermons held on this day. Additionally, the report will delve into the traditions and customs associated with Eid, such as the exchange of heartfelt gifts, the donning of new clothes, and the indulgence in festive meals. By understanding the significance of Eid al-Fitr, readers will gain a comprehensive understanding of the culmination of the Ramadan experience in Iraq.\

Lastly, this report aims to reflect on the profound impact of Ramadan on Iraqi society. It will delve into personal experiences and stories shared by individuals, highlighting the transformative lessons learned during Ramadan and the ways in which this holy month shapes the lives of individuals. Additionally, the report will examine the broader impact of Ramadan on Iraqi society, including its influence on social cohesion, community engagement, and the preservation of cultural heritage. By reflecting on the past and present, this report will also offer insights into the future of Ramadan traditions in Iraq, providing recommendations for further research and exploration.

In conclusion, the purpose of this report is to provide readers with a unique and comprehensive understanding of the Ramadan traditions in Iraq. By exploring the historical, cultural, and religious aspects of Ramadan, as well as the diverse customs and practices observed during this sacred month, readers will gain a deeper appreciation for the significance of Ramadan in Iraqi society. Through this report, readers will be able to immerse themselves in the vibrant tapestry of Iraqi Ramadan traditions and gain a greater understanding of the cultural heritage that shapes the Iraqi people's experience during this sacred month.

METHODOLOGY

To ensure a comprehensive exploration of Ramadan traditions in Iraq, a combination of primary and secondary research methods was employed for this report. Primary research involved conducting interviews with individuals who possess firsthand experience and knowledge of Ramadan traditions in Iraq. The interviewees consisted of a diverse group, including religious scholars, community leaders, and ordinary Iraqis who actively observe Ramadan.

These interviews were conducted through various means such as in-person, phone calls, and online platforms, allowing for a wide range of perspectives to be included in the research. The questions posed during the interviews focused on different aspects of Ramadan traditions, including the preparations lead-ing up to Ramadan, fasting practices, family and community gatherings, and the significance of Laylat al-Qadr and Eid al-Fitr.

In addition to interviews, valuable insights were gained through observations made during the month of Ramadan in different regions of Iraq. These observations took place in mosques, homes, and community centers, providing a comprehensive understanding of the diverse traditions and customs followed by Iraqis during Ramadan.

To supplement the primary research findings, secondary re-search was conducted. This involved a thorough review of academic articles, books, and online resources to gather information on the historical and cultural background of Ramadan in Iraq. This secondary research helped provide a broader context for understanding the significance of Ramadan in Iraqi culture and its evolution over time.

Furthermore, various government publications, religious texts, and media sources were consulted to gather information on the official announcements of Ramadan, the religious guidelines for fasting, and the various community events and activities that take place during this month.

By employing a combination of primary and secondary research methods, this report aims to present a comprehensive and well-rounded understanding of Ramadan traditions in Iraq. The inclusion of multiple sources and perspectives ensures an accurate and insightful portrayal of the customs and practices followed by Iraqis during this important month.

It is important to acknowledge that cultural practices and traditions can vary among different regions and communities within Iraq. Therefore, while every effort has been made to ensure the accuracy of the information presented in this report, the findings should be considered as a general overview of Ramadan traditions in Iraq and may not encompass the full diversity of practices observed throughout the country.

In the following chapters, the research findings will be presented in detail, providing readers with a comprehensive understanding of the background, significance, and various aspects of Ramadan traditions in Iraq.

PREPARATION FOR RAMADAN

ANNOUNCEMENT OF RAMADAN IN IRAQ

The anticipation and excitement surrounding the announcement of Ramadan in Iraq make it a highly anticipated event for Muslims across the country. Various methods are employed to ensure that everyone is aware of the beginning of the holy month.

Moon Sighting

The sighting of the new moon is the most common method used to announce the start of Ramadan in Iraq. Islamic scholars and religious authorities carefully observe the sky on the 29th day of the previous month to search for the crescent moon. Once the moon is sighted, it signifies the commencement of Ramadan. Religious authorities then confirm the sighting and make the official announcement.

Role of Religious Authorities

Religious authorities play a crucial role in announcing Ramadan in Iraq. They are responsible for verifying the moon sighting and making the official declaration. These authorities include esteemed scholars, imams, and religious organizations. Their announcement holds great significance and is widely respected and followed by the Muslim community.

Government Involvement

In addition to the announcement made by religious authorities, the Iraqi government also plays a role in informing the public about the start of Ramadan. The Ministry of Religious Affairs and Endowments collaborates with religious authorities to make an official announcement. This ensures that the entire population, regardless of their religious affiliation, is aware of the beginning of Ramadan.

Media and Social Media

With the advancement of technology, the announcement of Ramadan in Iraq has embraced modern means of communication. The media, including television, radio, and newspapers, play a significant role in spreading the news of Ramadan's arrival. Special programs and articles are dedicated to informing the public about the commencement of the holy month. Social media platforms such as Facebook, Twitter, and Instagram are also utilized to share the announcement, enabling people to quickly disseminate the news among their friends and family.

Mosques and Community Engagement

Mosques and community centers play a vital role in disseminating the announcement of Ramadan. Imams and religious leaders make the announcement during Friday sermons and other congregational prayers. They inform worshippers about the start of Ramadan and emphasize the importance of fasting and engaging in acts of worship during this blessed month. Community centers also organize events and gatherings to celebrate the beginning of Ramadan, further spreading the news among the community.

Public Celebrations

The announcementof Ramadan in Iraq is often accompanied by public celebrations, adding to the joyous atmosphere. People come together in public spaces such as parks and squares to mark the beginning of the holy month. These celebrations feature traditional music, captivating dance performances, and the distribution of symbolic sweets and dates. The air is filled with excitement and a sense of unity as individuals gather to celebrate the auspicious start of Ramadan.

In conclusion, the announcement of Ramadan in Iraq is a highly anticipated event that holds great significance for the Muslim community. It is conveyed through various channels, including moon sighting, religious authorities, government involvement, media, social media, mosques, and community engagement. The announcement not only signifies the commencement of Ramadan but also serves as a time of celebration and togetherness among the people of Iraq.

PREPARING FOR RAMADAN: THE JOY OF SHOPPING

The anticipation of Ramadan in Iraq is accompanied by the

excitement of pre-Ramadan shopping. It is a time when families and individuals eagerly gather essential items and delightful treats to ensure a seamless and enjoyable month of fasting and celebration.

The Significance of Pre-Ramadan Shopping

Pre-Ramadan shopping holds great importance in the overall preparation for the holy month. It allows individuals to gather all the necessary items they will need during Ramadan, ensuring they are well-equipped and can fully focus on their spiritual journey without any distractions. Moreover, it adds to the sense of anticipation and enthusiasm as people eagerly await the upcoming month of fasting and worship.

Traditional Items for Pre-Ramadan Shopping

1. **Food and Beverages**: Pre-Ramadan shopping centers around stocking up on food and beverages that will be consumed during Suhoor (pre-dawn meal) and Iftar (meal to break the fast). Traditional Iraqi delicacies like samoon (a type of bread), dates, olives, yogurt, and an assortment of sweets are commonly purchased. Families also acquire ingredients for special Ramadan recipes they plan to prepare during the month.
2. **Dates**: Dates hold immense significance during Ramadan, as they are traditionally the first food to be consumed to break the fast. Therefore, it is customary for people to purchase ample quantities of dates to ensure an abundant supply throughout the month.
3. **Water and Refreshments**: Given that fasting in Iraq

often coincides with the hot summer months, it is crucial to have an ample supply of water and other refreshing beverages. People stock up on bottled water, juices, and traditional drinks like jallab and tamarind juice.

4. **Household Supplies**: Alongside food and beverages, individuals also acquire household supplies to ensure a clean and comfortable environment during Ramadan. Cleaning products, toiletries, and other essentials are purchased in advance to avoid any last-minute rush.

5. **New Attire**: Many families consider it a tradition to purchase new clothes for themselves and their children before the start of Ramadan. This practice adds to the festive atmosphere and allows individuals to feel their best during the month of fasting and celebration.

Shopping Rituals and Customs

Pre-Ramadan shopping in Iraq is not merely a transactional experience; it is a social and cultural event. People often visit bustling local markets and shops that are adorned with special Ramadan promotions. These markets offer a wide variety of goods, including food, clothing, home decor, and religious items.

Families often embark on the shopping journey together, turning it into a bonding experience. Parents involve their children in the process, imparting knowledge about the significance of Ramadan and the items they are purchasing. This fosters a sense of tradition and cultural values in the younger generation, strengthening the connection to their heritage.

Economic Impact of Pre-Ramadan Shopping

The month of Ramadan serves as a peak period for businesses in Iraq, particularly those in the food and retail sectors. Pre-Ramadan shopping significantly contributes to the local economy as people increase their spending on groceries, clothing, and other goods during this time. It provides a much-needed boost to small businesses and vendors who rely on the heightened demand to generate income and support their livelihoods.

Pre-Ramadan shopping in Iraq is a time filled with anticipation and preparation for the holy month. It involves gathering essential items, stocking up on traditional foods, and acquiring new clothes. This ritual not only ensures a smooth and enjoyable Ramadan experience but also plays a vital role in stimulating the local economy. The practice of pre-Ramadan shopping reflects the cultural and social significance of Ramadan in Iraqi society, fostering a sense of unity and excitement as the community prepares to embark on this sacred journey together.

HOUSE CLEANING AND DECORATION

Preparing the house through cleaning and decoration holds great significance in the lead-up to Ramadan in Iraq. This section delves into the importance of this practice and explores the traditional customs associated with it.

The Significance of Cleaning

Cleaning the house before Ramadan is considered both a physical and spiritual preparation for the month of fasting and devotion. It is believed that a clean and organized home fosters a peaceful and serene atmosphere, conducive to spiritual reflection and worship. The act of cleaning is seen as a means of purifying oneself and the surroundings, promoting a sense of purity and tranquility.

Thorough Cleaning

In the weeks preceding Ramadan, families engage in a comprehensive cleaning of their homes. This entails dusting, sweeping, mopping, and decluttering every nook and cranny. It is a time-consuming task that involves the active participation of all family members. The thorough cleaning process aims to eliminate impurities and negative energy from the house, creating a clean and sacred space for the holy month.

Decluttering and Organization

During the cleaning process, families take the opportunity to declutter and organize their belongings. Unwanted items are discarded, while the remaining possessions are neatly arranged. This practice not only promotes a sense of order but also cultivates gratitude for the blessings one possesses. A clutter-free environment is believed to foster a focused and peaceful mindset during Ramadan.

House Decoration

Once the cleaning is complete, families shift their focus to decorating the house in preparation for Ramadan. This is done to create a festive and joyful ambiance that reflects the significance of the holy month. Traditional decorations include vibrant lanterns, known as "fanoos," which are hung in windows and doorways. These lanterns symbolize the guiding light of Ramadan and are a common sight throughout the country.

Ramadan-inspired Decor

In addition to lanterns, families adorn their homes with other Ramadan-themed items. This may include banners featuring religious verses or quotes, colorful fabrics, and artwork depicting Islamic calligraphy or symbols. The aim is to establish a visually captivating and spiritually uplifting environment that serves as a constant reminder of the importance of Ramadan.

Special Areas of the House

Certain areas of the house receive special attention during the cleaning and decoration process. The prayer area, known as the "musalla," is meticulously prepared to provide a dedicated space for worship and reflection. It is adorned with prayer rugs, cushions, and religious texts. The dining area, where the family gathers for iftar and suhoor, is also given special consideration in terms of decoration. Tablecloths, candles, and special dinnerware are used to create a festive ambiance, enhancing the dining experience during Ramadan.

Involvement of Children

Cleaning and decorating the house for Ramadan is a family affair, and children actively participate in the process. They are encouraged to engage in age-appropriate tasks such as dusting, arranging cushions, or assisting with decorations. This not only teaches them the importance of cleanliness and organization but also instills a sense of responsibility and ownership in preparing for the holy month. It becomes a valuable opportunity for children to learn about the significance of Ramadan traditions and actively contribute to the family's preparations.

Cleaning and decorating the house before Ramadan is a cherished tradition in Iraq, symbolizing the anticipation and reverence for the holy month. It serves as a physical and spiritual preparation, creating a clean and welcoming environment for fasting and worship. The act of cleaning promotes a sense of purity and tranquility, while the decorations evoke a festive atmosphere that reflects the joy and significance of Ramadan. This practice not only enhances the visual appeal of the house but also fosters unity and devotion among family members. By involving children in these preparations, the tradition is passed down through generations, reinforcing the values and customs associated with Ramadan in Iraq.

UNIQUE FLAVORS OF RAMADAN: IRAQ CULINARY DELIGHTS

Ramadan, a time of spiritual reflection and self-discipline, is celebrated by Muslims worldwide, including in Iraq. This sacred month involves fasting from dawn until sunset, where Muslims abstain from food and drink. However, as the sun sets, families and communities come together to break their fast with a special meal known as iftar. In Iraq, iftar is a time of celebration and togetherness, and it is marked by the preparation and consumption of unique and flavorful Ramadan recipes.

Traditional Iraqi Cuisine: A Tapestry of Flavors

Iraqi cuisine is renowned for its rich flavors and diverse ingredients, and during Ramadan, traditional dishes take center stage. These recipes have been passed down through generations, weaving a tapestry of flavors that reflect the country's cultural heritage. Let's explore some of the distinctive Ramadan recipes that are commonly prepared in Iraq:

Samoon: The Pillowy Bread

Samoon, a traditional Iraqi bread, is a staple during iftar. This pillowy bread boasts a soft and fluffy texture with a slightly crispy crust. Made from a simple dough of flour, yeast, salt, and water, it is shaped into oval or round loaves before being baked to perfection. Samoon is often served with delightful accompaniments such as hummus, baba ganoush, or falafel, enhancing the iftar experience.

Dolma: Stuffed Vegetable Delights

Dolma, a beloved dish in Iraq, takes on a special significance during Ramadan. It features a medley of stuffed vegetables, including bell peppers, zucchini, or grape leaves. The filling, a delightful blend of rice, ground meat, onions, herbs, and spices, creates a burst of flavors. Cooked in a flavorful tomato-based sauce until tender, dolma is a nutritious and delicious dish cherished by all generations during Ramadan.

Tashreeb: A Hearty Soup for Nourishment

Tashreeb, a traditional Iraqi soup, warms the hearts and nourishes the bodies of those breaking their fast during iftar. This hearty dish consists of pieces of bread soaked in a flavorful broth. The broth, often made with chicken or lamb, is infused with a combination of onions, carrots, and celery to create a comforting and aromatic flavor. Seasoned with a blend of spices and herbs, Tashreeb provides a satisfying and nourishing start to the iftar meal.

Quzi: A Festive Lamb and Rice Delicacy

Quzi, a dish synonymous with celebration, takes center stage during special occasions, including Ramadan. This traditional Iraqi lamb and rice dish is cooked with an array of aromatic spices and herbs. The lamb is slow-cooked to perfection, resulting in tender and flavorful meat that is served on a bed of fragrant rice. Garnished with roasted nuts and accompanied by a side of yogurt or salad, Quzi brings families together in joyous celebration during Ramadan.

Kleicha: Sweet Pastry Delights

Kleicha, a beloved Iraqi pastry, holds a special place in the hearts and palates of those observing Ramadan. These sweet treats are filled with a delightful mixture of dates, nuts, or sweetened coconut. The dough, made with a combination of flour, butter, sugar, and yeast, is skillfully rolled out and filled with the desired ingredients. Kleicha is then shaped into various forms, such as crescents or rectangles, and baked until golden brown. Paired with a cup of tea or Arabic coffee, Kleicha adds a touch of sweetness to the iftar experience.

Modern Innovations: A Twist on Tradition

While traditional recipes continue to be cherished, modern innovations have emerged, adding a unique twist to Iraqi Ramadan cuisine. Chefs and home cooks have begun experimenting with flavors and techniques, infusing international influences and fusion flavors into their creations. These modern recipes offer a fresh and exciting culinary experience during Ramadan.

Grilled Kebabs with a Contemporary Flair

Grilled kebabs, a beloved staple of Iraqi cuisine, have undergone a contemporary transformation during Ramadan. While traditional kebabs are made with ground meat and spices, modern variations introduce unique ingredients and flavor combinations. For instance, marinated chicken or lamb kebabs infused with Middle Eastern spices and served with a tangy yogurt sauce provide a refreshing twist on the classic dish.

Fusion Desserts: A Sweet Symphony

Desserts play a significant role in the iftar spread, and modern Ramadan recipes have elevated dessert innovation to new heights. Chefs have skillfully combined traditional Iraqi sweets with international flavors, creating fusion desserts that tantalize the taste buds and captivate the eyes. One popular example is the date and chocolate tart, where a buttery crust envelops a luscious chocolate ganache, topped with sweet dates. These fusion desserts add a touch of excitement and novelty to the Ramadan table, delighting both young and old.

Embracing Vegetarian Delights

In recent years, there has been a growing trend towards vegetarian and plant-based diets, and this influence has extended to Ramadan recipes in Iraq. Chefs and home cooks have embraced the challenge of creating vegetarian versions of traditional dishes. For instance, instead of using meat in dolma, some recipes now feature a filling made with a medley of rice, lentils, and vibrant vegetables. These vegetarian delights offer a lighter and healthier alternative for those observing Ramadan, while still delivering a burst of flavors.

Preserving Culinary Heritage: Passing Down the Recipes

One of the most beautiful aspects of Ramadan in Iraq is the passing down of recipes from one generation to another. Families take great pride in preserving their culinary heritage and ensuring that the special Ramadan recipes are carried forward. Grandmothers and mothers play a vital role in teaching their children and grandchildren the art of preparing these dishes, ensuring that the flavors and techniques are not lost over time. This tradition strengthens family bonds and creates a sense of continuity and connection to the past.

Conclusion: A Feast for the Senses

The unique flavors of Ramadan in Iraq, from traditional dishes to modern innovations, create a feast for the senses. These culinary delights bring families and communities together, fostering a sense of togetherness and celebration during this holy month. As the recipes are passed down through generations, the culinary heritage of Iraq continues to thrive, creating lasting memories and strengthening the bonds of love and tradition. Ramadan in Iraq is truly a time to savor the rich flavors and embrace the culinary treasures that make this month so special.

FASTING DURING RAMADAN

The Significance of Fasting

Fasting holds a profound significance within the Ramadan traditions of Iraq. It is a sacred time when Muslims willingly abstain from food, drink, and other physical needs from dawn until sunset. Considered one of the Five Pillars of Islam, fasting during Ramadan is a fundamental act of worship for Muslims.

A Path to Spiritual Purification

Fasting extends beyond the mere act of refraining from eating and drinking; it is a spiritual practice aimed at purifying the soul and strengthening the bond between individuals and Allah. This period serves as a time for self-reflection, self-discipline, and self-control. By detaching themselves from worldly desires, Muslims focus on their spiritual growth and seek forgiveness for their transgressions.

Cultivating Empathy and Compassion

Fasting during Ramadan also fosters empathy and compassion

towards those who are less fortunate. It serves as a reminder of the struggles faced by the impoverished and hungry, motivating Muslims to be more charitable and generous. Throughout this holy month, it is common to witness individuals and organizations distributing food and essential supplies to those in need.

Nurturing Self-Discipline

Fasting demands strong self-discipline and willpower. It teaches individuals to govern their desires and impulses, which can prove beneficial in all aspects of life. By practicing self-restraint during Ramadan, Muslims learn to resist temptations and develop a sense of discipline that can be applied to various areas, including work, relationships, and personal goals.

Physical and Mental Well-being

Fasting has been recognized for its numerous physical and mental benefits. It allows the digestive system to rest and rejuvenate, leading to improved digestion and detoxification of the body. Additionally, fasting promotes mental clarity and focus by eliminating distractions associated with food, enabling individuals to concentrate on their spiritual practices and daily activities.

Strengthening Faith and Connection with Allah

Fasting serves as a time of heightened devotion and worship. Muslims devote more time to prayer, recitation of the Quran, and contemplation of their faith. The act of fasting itself is viewed as an act of worship and a means of seeking closeness to Allah. It is believed that during Ramadan, the gates of heaven are open, and the rewards for good deeds are multiplied. This serves as a source of motivation for Muslims to engage in more acts of worship and seek spiritual growth.

Unity and Solidarity

Fasting during Ramadan fosters a sense of unity and solidarity among Muslims in Iraq. The entire community comes together to observe the fast, share meals, and participate in religious activities. It is a time when families and friends gather for iftar, the meal to break the fast, and engage in communal prayers. This sense of togetherness strengthens the bonds within the community and nurtures a spirit of brotherhood and sisterhood.

Personal Growth and Reflection

Ramadan provides a unique opportunity for personal growth and reflection. It allows individuals to assess their actions, seek forgiveness, and make positive changes in their lives. Muslims often set personal goals during this month, such as completing the recitation of the entire Quran, increasing acts of charity, or improving their character. The fasting period encourages introspection and self-improvement, leading to a renewed sense of purpose and spirituality.

In conclusion, fasting holds immense significance within the Ramadan traditions in Iraq. It serves as a pathway to spiritual purification, empathy, and self-discipline. Fasting strengthens the connection with Allah, promotes unity within the community, and fosters personal growth and reflection. It is not only a religious obligation but also a transformative experience that impacts the lives of individuals and the society as a whole.

SUHOOR AD IFTRE: NOURISHING MOMENTS OF TOGETHERNESS

Suhoor and Iftar, the two significant meals during the holy month of Ramadan in Iraq, hold a special place in the hearts of the Iraqi people. Suhoor, the pre-dawn meal, prepares individuals for the day of fasting ahead, while Iftar, the meal that breaks the fast at sunset, becomes a moment of joy and celebration for families and communities.

Suhoor: Energizing the Body and Soul

Suhoor, consumed before the break of dawn and the Fajr prayer, plays a vital role in providing sustenance throughout the day. In Iraq, Suhoor is a simple yet nourishing meal, carefully crafted to offer a balance of carbohydrates, proteins, and healthy fats. Traditional Iraqi bread, known as Samoon, takes center stage during Suhoor, accompanied by a delightful array of cheese, olives, and yogurt. Dates, a Middle Eastern staple, provide a quick source of energy and are commonly enjoyed during this meal. Foul medames (fava beans), eggs, and hearty porridge made from grains like barley or wheat are also popular choices.

Beyond the food itself, Suhoor becomes a time for families to come together, sharing not only a meal but also moments of reflection, prayer, and supplication. The early hours of the morning witness the unity and togetherness as families rise early to prepare and enjoy Suhoor, strengthening their bonds and fostering a sense of community.

Iftar: A Feast of Gratitude and Connection

Iftar, the eagerly awaited meal that breaks the fast at sunset, becomes a moment of celebration and gratitude for Muslims in Iraq. The melodious call to prayer, the Adhan, marks the end of the fast, and families gather around the table with anticipation.

In Iraq, Iftar is a grand affair, featuring a wide variety of dishes to satiate the hunger and quench the thirst of those who have been fasting all day. The breaking of the fast begins with the customary consumption of dates and water, following the tradition of the Prophet Muhammad (peace be upon him). Dates, with their natural sweetness, replenish the body's energy levels after a day of fasting.

After the initial dates and water, a more substantial meal unfolds, showcasing the rich flavors and aromas of traditional Iraqi cuisine. Tashreeb, a hearty bread soup, takes its place alongside Dolma, a delightful dish of stuffed vegetables like grape leaves or bell peppers. Biryani, kebabs, and an assortment of rice and meat dishes add to the culinary tapestry of Iftar in Iraq.

However, Iftar is not solely about indulging in delicious food; it is a time for prayer and gratitude as well. Following the Maghrib prayer, Muslims in Iraq express their appreciation to Allah for the sustenance provided. This is followed by a more elaborate meal, where families and friends gather to share stories, laughter, and the blessings of Ramadan.

The significance of Suhoor and Iftar extends beyond the physical nourishment they provide. These meals hold a deep cultural and spiritual meaning in Iraqi society. They serve as moments of unity, strengthening the bonds between family members and friends. Suhoor and Iftar foster a sense of togetherness and solidarity, reminding individuals of the values of self-discipline and self-control.

In essence, Suhoor and Iftar are not just about the food; they are about the shared experience of fasting and breaking the fast together as a community. These meals nourish not only the body but also the soul, as they are accompanied by prayers, reflection, and gratitude. Suhoor and Iftar are cherished traditions that contribute to the rich cultural tapestry of Iraq during the holy month of Ramadan. They symbolize the values of unity, gratitude, and the importance of coming together as a community to celebrate and honor this sacred time.

TRADITIONAL IRAQ DELICACIES FOR IFTAR

Iftar, the cherished meal that breaks the fast during Ramadan, holds a special place in the hearts of families and communities in Iraq. It is a time of unity and joy, accompanied by the indulgence of traditional Iraqi delicacies. The culinary heritage of Iraq, shaped by its history and culture, offers a diverse array of flavors. In this section, we will explore the mouthwatering traditional Iraqi dishes that are commonly prepared for iftar.

Samoon: The Fluffy Bread

Samoon, a staple in Iraqi cuisine, is a soft and fluffy bread with a delightful crispy crust. During Ramadan, the aroma of freshly baked samoon fills the air, adding to the festive ambiance. It is often served alongside various dishes such as stews, grilled meats, or used as a base for sandwiches. Breaking the warm samoon and savoring its taste is a cherished moment during iftar.

Dolma: Stuffed Vegetable Delight

Dolma, a beloved dish in Iraq, takes center stage during Ramadan. It involves stuffing vegetables like bell peppers, zucchini, or eggplant with a delectable mixture of rice, ground meat, herbs, and spices. These stuffed vegetables are then cooked in a tomato-based sauce until they reach a tender perfection. Though preparing dolma requires time and effort, the result is a rewarding main course for iftar, often accompanied by yogurt or a side salad.

Tashreeb: Hearty Bread Soup

Tashreeb, a traditional Iraqi dish, holds a special place during Ramadan. It is a hearty soup made by soaking pieces of bread in a flavorful broth. The broth, seasoned with spices like turmeric, cumin, and coriander, is typically prepared with lamb or chicken. Tashreeb provides comfort and nourishment, making it an ideal choice for breaking the fast. Garnished with fresh herbs, this hot soup is a delightful addition to the iftar table.

Quzi: The Festive Roasted Delicacy

Quzi, a dish reserved for special occasions including Ramadan, is a whole roasted lamb or goat stuffed with a fragrant mixture of rice, nuts, and spices. Slow-cooked until tender, the meat is served with a rich and flavorful sauce. Quzi symbolizes generosity and hospitality in Iraqi culture, making it a centerpiece dish shared among family and friends during iftar gatherings. The succulent flavors and tender meat of Quzi create a memorable and festive dining experience.

Baklava: Sweet Pastry Delight

Baklava, a beloved sweet pastry, holds a special place in Ramadan celebrations in Iraq. Layers of thin filo pastry are filled with a delightful mixture of nuts, such as pistachios or walnuts, and sweetened with a syrup made from honey or sugar. Baklava is known for its rich and indulgent flavors, making it a perfect dessert for iftar. The sweet and crunchy texture of Baklava provides a delightful ending to the meal, leaving a lasting impression.

Masgouf: Grilled Fish Delicacy

Masgouf, a traditional Iraqi dish, is often prepared for special occasions, including Ramadan. It involves grilling a whole fish, typically carp or catfish, marinated in a blend of spices over an open fire. The fish is then served with rice and a tangy sauce made from tamarind or lemon. Masgouf holds a special place during iftar, particularly in the southern regions of Iraq where freshwater fish are abundant. Its smoky and flavorful taste adds a unique touch to the Ramadan dining experience.

Jajeek: Refreshing Yogurt Salad

Jajeek, a refreshing yogurt and cucumber salad, is a common accompaniment during iftar in Iraq. Made with yogurt, cucumbers, garlic, and mint, it offers a cooling and tangy flavor that complements the rich and savory main dishes. Jajeek is often enjoyed with samoon or used as a topping for grilled meats, adding a refreshing element to the iftar spread.

Dates and Nuts: Traditional Delights

Dates and nuts hold a significant place in Iraqi iftar traditions. Dates, being the first food to be eaten to break the fast, are considered a practice of the Prophet Muhammad and hold symbolic importance. They provide a quick source of energy after a day of fasting due to their natural sugars. Nuts, such as almonds, walnuts, and pistachios, are also commonly served during iftar. They add a delightful crunch and are a good source of protein and healthy fats, enhancing the overall dining experience.

ACT OF CHARITY DURING RAMADAN

Ramadan in Iraq is not only a time of fasting and spiritual reflection but also a season of generosity and compassion. The Iraqi people embrace numerous charitable acts during this holy month, aiming to uplift the less fortunate and spread joy among those in need. These acts of charity hold deep roots in Islamic teachings and are an integral part of Ramadan traditions in

Iraq.

Zakat and Sadaqah: Giving for a Purpose

One of the most significant charitable acts during Ramadan in Iraq is the practice of Zakat and Sadaqah. Zakat, one of the Five Pillars of Islam, requires Muslims to donate a portion of their wealth to support those in need. Throughout Ramadan, many Iraqis fulfill their Zakat obligations by offering money, food, or essential items to the impoverished. This act of giving not only assists the less fortunate but also purifies the wealth of the giver.

Sadaqah, on the other hand, is voluntary charity that can be given at any time and in any amount. However, during Ramadan, the act of giving Sadaqah is highly encouraged and considered more rewarding. Many Iraqis seize this opportunity to give generously, supporting various charitable organizations and initiatives that provide assistance to those in need.

Sponsorship of Iftar and Suhoor: Nourishing the Community

Another prevalent charitable act during Ramadan in Iraq is the sponsorship of Iftar and Suhoor meals. Individuals, families, and organizations step forward to sponsor these meals for those who are unable to afford them. Mosques, community centers, and charitable organizations organize Iftar and Suhoor programs, where individuals and families can gather to break their fasts together. Sponsors provide the necessary food and drinks for these gatherings, ensuring that everyone can enjoy a nutritious meal during Ramadan.

Sponsoring Iftar and Suhoor meals not only provides physical nourishment but also fosters a sense of community and togetherness. It allows people from different backgrounds to come together and share the blessings of Ramadan, regardless of their financial circumstances.

Distribution of Food and Essential Items: Extending a Helping Hand

During Ramadan, many Iraqis engage in the distribution of food and essential items to those in need. This act of charity holds particular significance during the holy month, as it ensures that everyone has access to basic necessities. Individuals and organizations collect donations of food, clothing, hygiene products, and other essentials, which are then distributed to disadvantaged communities, orphanages, and refugee camps.

The distribution of food and essential items goes beyond material support. Many Iraqis also contribute to the preparation and distribution of cooked meals for those facing financial hardships during Ramadan. Volunteers come together to cook and distribute meals, ensuring that everyone can enjoy a fulfilling and nutritious meal.

Support for Orphans and Widows: Embracing the Vulnerable

Ramadan is a time when special attention is given to orphans and widows in Iraq. Charitable organizations and individuals focus their efforts on providing support and assistance to these vulnerable groups. Orphanages and shelters receive increased attention during Ramadan, with donations of money, food, clothing, and other necessities to ensure the well-being of the children and widows.

In addition to material support, efforts are made to create a sense of belonging and happiness for orphans and widows during Ramadan. Special events and activities, such as iftar gatherings, gift distributions, and recreational outings, are organized to bring joy to their lives. These acts of charity not only provide immediate relief but also contribute to the long-term well-being and development of these individuals.

Blood Donations: Saving Lives, Spreading Hope

Another significant charitable act during Ramadan in Iraq is blood donation. Many Iraqis recognize the importance of donating blood and saving lives, especially during a time when medical facilities may be overwhelmed. Blood donation drives are organized in various locations, including mosques, community centers, and hospitals, to encourage individuals to donate blood and help those in need.

Donating blood during Ramadan is considered highly virtuous and is believed to bring immense blessings. It is seen as a selfless act of giving and a means of supporting those who are suffering from illnesses or injuries. Many Iraqis actively participate in blood donation drives, understanding the critical role it plays in saving lives and supporting the healthcare system.

In conclusion, acts of charity during Ramadan in Iraq play a vital role in fostering compassion, empathy, and solidarity within the community. The practice of Zakat and Sadaqah, sponsorship of Iftar and Suhoor meals, distribution of food and essential items, support for orphans and widows, and blood donations reflect the true spirit of Ramadan. These acts not only provide immediate relief to those in need but also strengthen the bonds of brotherhood and contribute to the overall well-being of Iraqi society. Through these acts of charity, the Iraqi people demonstrate their commitment to the values of compassion, generosity, and unity that Ramadan embodies. As the holy month continues to be celebrated in Iraq, these charitable traditions will continue to uplift communities, bring hope to the less fortunate, and leave a lasting impact on the hearts and minds of all those involved.

TARAWEEH PRAYERS: A SPIRITUAL JOURNEY IN IRAQ

Taraweeh prayers hold a special place in the hearts of Muslims in Iraq during the holy month of Ramadan. These prayers, performed after the Isha prayer, play a significant role in the spiritual journey of individuals and the community as a whole. In this section, we will delve into the significance of Taraweeh prayers in Iraqi culture, the rituals observed during these prayers, and the profound impact they have on the community.

The Significance of Taraweeh Prayers

Taraweeh prayers are highly revered by Muslims in Iraq as they offer a unique opportunity for increased devotion and connection with Allah. The term "Taraweeh" derives from the Arabic word "taraweeh," meaning to rest and relax. These congregational prayers are known for their extended recitation of the Quran, allowing worshippers to immerse themselves in its verses.

The significance of Taraweeh prayers lies in the belief that they provide a chance to seek forgiveness, gain spiritual strength, and earn abundant rewards from Allah. During Ramadan, it is believed that the gates of heaven are open, and the blessings for good deeds are multiplied. Therefore, Muslims in Iraq eagerly participate in Taraweeh prayers to maximize their spiritual growth and draw closer to Allah.

Rituals and Practices

Taraweeh prayers take place in mosques across Iraq, where the community gathers to engage in this collective act of worship. Led by an Imam, the prayers involve the melodious and captivating recitation of the Quran. The recitation is divided into portions, known as "rak'ahs," and can span over several nights, with the entire Quran being completed by the end of Ramadan.

The atmosphere in the mosque during Taraweeh prayers is serene and filled with devotion. Worshippers stand shoulder to shoulder, following the movements and recitation of the Imam. Many individuals bring their personal copies of the Quran to follow along, while others listen attentively, absorbing the beauty of the verses being recited.

Taraweeh prayers often incorporate supplications and remembrance of Allah, adding an additional layer of spirituality. This allows individuals to reflect on their actions, seek forgiveness, and offer heartfelt prayers for themselves, their loved ones, and the entire Muslim community.

Community Impact

Taraweeh prayers not only have a personal impact on individuals but also foster a sense of unity and community among Muslims in Iraq. The collective nature of these prayers brings people together, strengthening the bonds of brotherhood and sisterhood.

Mosques become vibrant centers of activity during Ramadan, with people from all walks of life coming together to perform Taraweeh prayers. This communal experience creates a sense of belonging and solidarity, as individuals share in the spiritual journey of Ramadan.

Taraweeh prayers also provide an opportunity for individuals to connect with their local community and build relationships. After the prayers, people often engage in conversations, exchange greetings, and share meals together. This fosters a sense of camaraderie and promotes a spirit of generosity and kindness.

Personal Reflection and Spiritual Growth

For many Muslims in Iraq, Taraweeh prayers serve as a time for personal reflection and spiritual growth. The extended recitation of the Quran allows individuals to immerse themselves in the beauty and wisdom of the divine words. It provides a chance to ponder over the verses, seek guidance, and strengthen their relationship with Allah.

The peaceful and serene environment of the mosque during Taraweeh prayers offers a respite from the hustle and bustle of daily life. It allows individuals to disconnect from worldly distractions and focus solely on their connection with Allah. This dedicated time for worship and reflection helps individuals gain a deeper understanding of their faith and encourages them to strive for self-improvement.

Conclusion

Taraweeh prayers hold immense significance in the lives of Muslims in Iraq during the holy month of Ramadan. They provide a platform for increased devotion, personal reflection, and community bonding. The rituals and practices associated with Taraweeh prayers create an atmosphere of spirituality and unity, fostering a sense of belonging and shared purpose. Through these prayers, individuals in Iraq find solace, seek forgiveness, and strive for spiritual growth, making Taraweeh prayers an integral part of Ramadan traditions in Iraq.

QURAN RECITATION AND REFLECTION: NOURISH-ING THE SOUL

Quran recitation and reflection hold a profound significance within the Ramadan traditions of Iraq. This sacred month is not only a time for fasting and prayer but also a period of deep spiritual introspection and connection with the Quran. In Iraq, as in many other parts of the world, Muslims devote a considerable amount of time during Ramadan to reciting and studying the Quran.

Embracing the Importance of Quran Recitation

The Quran is revered as the divine word of Allah, revealed to the Prophet Muhammad (peace be upon him). It serves as a source of guidance, wisdom, and spiritual nourishment for Muslims. During Ramadan, the significance of Quran recitation is heightened, as it is believed that the rewards for good deeds are multiplied during this blessed month.

In Iraq, Muslims recognize the importance of reciting the Quran during Ramadan and make a conscious effort to engage with its verses. They believe that reciting the Quran not only brings them closer to Allah but also purifies their hearts and minds. It is seen as a means of seeking forgiveness, acquiring knowledge, and finding solace in the words of Allah.

Daily Devotion to Quran Recitation

In Iraq, it is customary for individuals to set aside specific time each day for Quran recitation. Many people choose to recite the entire Quran over the course of Ramadan, dividing it into equal portions to be recited each day. This practice, known as "Khatm al-Quran," is considered a highly virtuous act.

Families often gather in the evenings to recite the Quran collectively, fostering a sense of unity and spirituality within the household. This practice not only strengthens family bonds but also encourages children to participate and learn from their elders, nurturing a love for the Quran from a young age.

Taraweeh Prayers and the Beauty of Quran Recitation

Taraweeh prayers hold a significant place in the Ramadan traditions of Iraq. These special congregational prayers are performed after the Isha prayer. During Taraweeh, a portion of the Quran is recited each night, with the aim of completing the entire Quran by the end of Ramadan. The recitation is often led by a knowledgeable imam, whose melodious tones captivate the hearts of the worshippers.

Muslims in Iraq eagerly attend Taraweeh prayers, not only to fulfill their religious obligations but also to immerse themselves in the recitation of the Quran. The soothing and melodious recitation creates a serene atmosphere, allowing individuals to reflect on the verses and connect with the message of Allah.

Reflecting and Contemplating the Divine Words

Quran recitation is not merely a mechanical act of reading the words; it is a time for deep reflection and contemplation. In Iraq, Muslims understand the importance of pondering over the meanings of the verses and applying them to their daily lives.

During Ramadan, individuals seize the opportunity to reflect on their actions, seek forgiveness for their shortcomings, and strive for personal growth. The Quran serves as a guide, providing moral and ethical principles that shape their behavior and interactions with others. It encourages them to be compassionate, just, and mindful of their responsibilities as Muslims.

Engaging in Quranic Study Circles and Tafsir Sessions

In addition to individual recitation and reflection, many communities in Iraq organize Quranic study circles and Tafsir (interpretation) sessions during Ramadan. These gatherings bring together individuals who are eager to deepen their understanding of the Quran and learn from scholars and knowledgeable individuals.

In these study circles, participants engage in discussions about the meanings and interpretations of the Quranic verses. They explore the historical context, linguistic nuances, and practical applications of the teachings. These sessions provide a platform for intellectual growth, fostering a deeper connection with the Quran and promoting a sense of unity among the participants.

The Profound Spiritual Impact

The recitation and reflection on the Quran during Ramadan have a profound spiritual impact on individuals in Iraq. It is a time of self-reflection, self-improvement, and seeking closeness to Allah. The recitation of the Quran and contemplation of its verses instill a sense of peace, tranquility, and spiritual fulfillment.

Through the recitation and reflection on the Quran, Muslims in Iraq find solace and guidance in their daily lives. It strengthens their faith, deepens their understanding of Islam, and reinforces their commitment to living a righteous and virtuous life. The

Quran becomes a source of inspiration, providing them with the strength and motivation to overcome challenges and strive for excellence.

In conclusion, Quran recitation and reflection are integral components of Ramadan traditions in Iraq. Muslims in Iraq dedicate time each day to recite the Quran, individually and collectively, seeking spiritual nourishment and guidance. The recitation is accompanied by deep reflection, contemplation, and study, allowing individuals to connect with the message of Allah and apply its teachings in their lives. This practice not only strengthens their faith but also fosters a sense of unity and community among Muslims in Iraq during the holy month of Ramadan.

The Quran, with its profound wisdom and divine guidance, serves as a beacon of light during Ramadan and beyond. It is a source of solace, inspiration, and moral compass for Muslims in Iraq, shaping their thoughts, actions, and interactions with others. Through the recitation and reflection on the Quran, they find spiritual fulfillment, deepen their understanding of Islam, and strive to embody its teachings in their daily lives.

As the month of Ramadan unfolds in Iraq, the recitation and contemplation of the Quran continue to nourish the souls of believers, fostering a deep connection with Allah and strengthening their commitment to righteousness. It is a time of introspection, self-improvement, and seeking closeness to the Divine. May the Quran's timeless wisdom continue to guide and inspire Muslims in Iraq and around the world during this blessed month and beyond.

FAMILY AND COMMUNITY GATHERINGS

Iftar Gatherings: A Time of Unity and Generosity

Iftar, the meal that marks the end of the daily fast during Ramadan, holds a special place in the hearts of Iraqis. It is a time when families and friends come together to celebrate, strengthen bonds, and foster a sense of community. The significance of iftar gatherings in Iraqi culture cannot be overstated.

The Significance of Iftar Gatherings

Iftar gatherings play a vital role in Iraqi culture, serving as a means for loved ones to reconnect and spend quality time together. Beyond the act of breaking the fast, these gatherings provide an opportunity for meaningful conversations and shared experiences. The Prophet Muhammad (peace be upon him) emphasized the importance of sharing food and hospitality during Ramadan, stating that those who provide iftar to a fasting person will be rewarded without diminishing the reward of the fasting individual.

Preparing for Iftar Gatherings

Preparations for iftar gatherings begin early in the day, as families lovingly prepare a variety of delicious dishes. Traditional Iraqi recipes, passed down through generations, are brought to life with aromatic spices and flavors. The table is adorned with an array of dishes, including dates, fresh fruits, soups, salads, main courses, and delectable desserts. Traditional Iraqi delicacies such as biryani, dolma, and masgouf often take center stage, showcasing the rich culinary heritage of Iraq.

Breaking the Fast Together

As the call to prayer signals the end of the fasting day, families eagerly gather around the table, eagerly anticipating the moment to break their fast. Following the example of the Prophet Muhammad (peace be upon him), the first date is traditionally consumed, accompanied by a sip of water or a refreshing glass of juice. The atmosphere during iftar is filled with gratitude and joy, as prayers are offered, expressing gratitude for the blessings of the day and the opportunity to share this meal with loved ones. Breaking the fast together creates a sense of unity and strengthens the bonds of family and friendship.

Sharing Meals and Stories

During iftar gatherings, meals are shared generously and with love. It is customary for families to extend invitations to neighbors, friends, and even strangers, embodying the spirit of hospitality deeply rooted in Iraqi culture. As the meal progresses, stories are shared, laughter fills the room, and conversations flow freely. Iftar becomes a time for families to catch up on each other's lives, share experiences, and create lasting memories. The joy of iftar gatherings extends beyond the meal itself, as it becomes a cherished opportunity for bonding and strengthening relationships.

Traditions and Customs

Iftar gatherings in Iraq are not solely centered around food; they are also accompanied by various traditions and customs. One such tradition is the recitation of the Quran before and after the meal. Families gather together to recite verses from the holy book, seeking blessings and spiritual enlightenment. This practice adds a profound sense of spirituality to the gathering, deepening the connection with faith.

Another cherished tradition is the exchange of gifts and sweets among family members and friends. This gesture symbolizes love, respect, and the spirit of giving during Ramadan. It serves as a heartfelt expression of gratitude and further strengthens the bonds of kinship and friendship.

Conclusion

Iftar gatherings with family and friends hold a significant place in the hearts of Iraqis. They provide a precious opportunity to come together, share meals, and strengthen the bonds of love and friendship. These gatherings nourish not only the body but also the soul, as they are filled with gratitude, joy, and a sense of community. The traditions and customs associated with iftar gatherings add depth and meaning to the experience, making it a cherished and integral part of Ramadan in Iraq. Through the act of breaking the fast together, Iraqis embrace unity, generosity, and the spirit of Ramadan.

MOSQUE ACTIVITIES AND COMMUNITY EVENTS

Mosques hold a special place in the hearts of Iraqis during the sacred month of Ramadan. They serve not only as places of worship but also as vibrant community centers where a variety of activities and events take place. These mosque activities and community events bring people together, fostering unity, spiritual growth, and social interaction.

Taraweeh Prayers

One of the most significant mosque activities during Ramadan is the observance of Taraweeh prayers. These prayers are performed after the Isha prayer and involve reciting lengthy portions of the Quran. Led by a knowledgeable and skilled reciter, known as the Imam, the Taraweeh prayers are conducted in congregation, attracting numerous worshippers.

The atmosphere within the mosque during Taraweeh prayers is serene and tranquil. The melodious recitation of the Quran, combined with the unity of the worshippers, creates an ambiance of peace and spirituality. People gather to listen to the beautiful recitation, reflect upon the verses of the Quran, and seek blessings and forgiveness from Allah.

Islamic Lectures and Sermons

Mosques also organize Islamic lectures and sermons through-out Ramadan. These enlightening sessions are delivered by knowledgeable scholars and religious leaders who provide guidance and insights into various aspects of Islam. The topics covered range from the significance of fasting to the importance of charity and good deeds during Ramadan.

These lectures and sermons serve as a source of education and inspiration for worshippers. They deepen their understanding of religious teachings and encourage individuals to strengthen their faith and engage in righteous actions. The mosque becomes a hub of learning and spiritual growth, where people come together to acquire knowledge and seek guidance.

Community Iftars

Another integral part of mosque activities during Ramadan is the organization of community iftars. Iftar is the meal that Muslims have to break their fast at sunset. Many mosques arrange communal iftar meals, where people gather to break their fast together. These community iftars promote unity and solidarity among worshippers.

Community iftars are often held in large tents or designated areas within the mosque premises. Volunteers generously contribute their time and resources to prepare the meals for the worshippers. The iftar meals typically consist of traditional Iraqi dishes, such as biryani, kebabs, and a variety of sweets.

During these community iftars, people from diverse back-grounds and social classes come together to share a meal and engage in meaningful conversations. It is a time for families, friends, and neighbors to connect and strengthen their bonds. The atmosphere is filled with joy and gratitude as people break their fast and express their appreciation for the blessings of Ramadan.

Nightly Prayers and Tahajjud

In addition to the Taraweeh prayers, mosques also hold nightly prayers and Tahajjud during Ramadan. Nightly prayers are performed after the Taraweeh prayers and consist of additional voluntary prayers. These prayers provide an opportunity for worshippers to seek closeness to Allah and engage in extra acts of worship.

Tahajjud prayers, on the other hand, are performed in the last third of the night and are highly recommended during Ramadan. Many mosques organize special programs for Tahajjud prayers, where worshippers gather in the late hours of the night to pray together. These prayers are considered a time of deep reflection, supplication, and seeking forgiveness.

The mosque becomes a place of spiritual rejuvenation during the nightly prayers and Tahajjud. The worshippers immerse themselves in prayer, recitation of the Quran, and personal reflection. The peaceful ambiance of the mosque, coupled with the collective devotion of the worshippers, creates a profound spiritual experience.

Quran Recitation Competitions

Mosques in Iraq also host Quran recitation competitions during Ramadan. These competitions aim to encourage the memorization and recitation of the Quran among the youth. Participants showcase their skills in reciting the Quran with proper pronunciation, intonation, and rhythm.

The Quran recitation competitions not only promote a love for the Quran but also provide a platform for young individuals to display their talent and dedication. Held within the mosque premises, participants are judged by a panel of experts in Quran recitation. Winners are awarded prizes and recognition for their efforts.

These competitions attract a large audience, including family members, friends, and community members. The atmosphere is filled with excitement and anticipation as participants take turns reciting verses from the Quran. The competitions not only foster healthy competition but also inspire others to engage in the recitation and study of the Quran.

In conclusion, mosques in Iraq play a vital role in organizing various activities and events during the holy month of Ramadan. From Taraweeh prayers to community iftars and Quran recitation competitions, these mosque activities bring people together, fostering unity, spiritual growth, and social interaction.

VISITING LOVED ONES AND EMBRACING COMMUNITY

Visiting loved ones and embracing the community during the

holy month of Ramadan holds immense significance in Iraqi culture. It is a time when families and neighbors come together, reinforcing their bonds and sharing in the blessings of this sacred time. This cherished tradition reflects the values of hospitality, generosity, and a strong sense of community spirit.

Strengthening Family Connections

Ramadan serves as a beautiful opportunity for families to re-connect and strengthen their ties. It is customary for extended family members to gather for iftar, the meal that breaks the fast at sunset. Relatives from near and far come together to share a meal, exchange stories, and catch up on each other's lives. This tradition not only fosters a sense of unity and belonging but also allows younger generations to learn from their elders and carry forward the customs and traditions of their ancestors.

Fostering Community Unity

In addition to visiting relatives, Iraqis also make a concerted effort to connect with their neighbors during Ramadan. It is customary to exchange greetings and well wishes with those living nearby. This practice helps foster a sense of community and solidarity, as neighbors come together to support and celebrate with one another during this special time. It is not uncommon for neighbors to invite each other for iftar or share homemade sweets and treats as a gesture of goodwill.

Sharing Nourishment and Kindness

During Ramadan, Iraqis often prepare extra food and share it with their loved ones and neighbors. This act of generosity is seen as a way to spread blessings and ensure that everyone has enough to eat during the month of fasting. Families take pride in preparing traditional Iraqi dishes such as biryani, dolma, and samoon bread, which they distribute to their loved ones and neighbors. Additionally, exchanging gifts, particularly with children, adds to the joyous atmosphere of Ramadan.

Seeking Blessings and Reconciliation

Visiting relatives and neighbors during Ramadan is not only about socializing and sharing meals; it is also a time for seeking blessings and reconciliation. It is believed that visiting the elderly and seeking their blessings brings good fortune and blessings to the entire family. Similarly, seeking forgiveness from relatives and neighbors for any past misunderstandings or grievances is considered an important act of spiritual purification during this holy month.

Promoting Interfaith Harmony

Ramadan provides a unique opportunity for people of different faiths to come together and celebrate shared values of compassion, empathy, and unity. In Iraq, a country known for its diverse religious and ethnic communities, this month fosters interfaith relations. Muslims often extend invitations to their non-Muslim neighbors and friends to join them for iftar, promoting interfaith dialogue and understanding. This practice not only strengthens bonds within the community but also promotes harmony and mutual respect among different religious communities in Iraq.

Instilling Values in the Next Generation

Visiting loved ones and neighbors during Ramadan also serves as a valuable teaching moment for children. Parents often bring their children along when visiting relatives, allowing them to witness firsthand the importance of maintaining strong family connections and fostering relationships with neighbors. This experience helps children develop a sense of empathy and understanding towards others, instilling in them the values that lie at the core of Ramadan traditions.

In conclusion, the tradition of visiting loved ones and embracing the community during Ramadan is deeply ingrained in Iraqi culture. It serves as a means to strengthen family bonds, build a sense of unity within the community, and promote interfaith harmony. This cherished practice brings joy and happiness to individuals and families while fostering a strong sense of solidarity within Iraqi society.

RAMADAN CUSTOMS AND CHILDREN

Ramadan holds a special place for families in Iraq, and children actively participate in the observance of this sacred month. They are entrusted with carrying forward traditions and values, ensuring the spirit of Ramadan thrives in the younger generation. In this section, we will explore the unique customs specifically tailored for children during Ramadan in Iraq.

Instilling the Significance of Fasting

Teaching children the importance of fasting is a fundamental tradition during Ramadan. Parents and elders take the time to explain the deeper meaning behind abstaining from food and drink from sunrise to sunset. They emphasize that fasting is not solely about refraining from eating but also about cultivating self-discipline, empathy, and gratitude. Children are encouraged to gradually fast for a few hours, gradually increasing the duration as they mature.

Engaging in Special Ramadan Activities

To make Ramadan more enjoyable and engaging for children, a variety of special activities are organized. Storytelling sessions are held, where children gather to listen to religious stories and learn valuable lessons. Arts and crafts workshops allow children to create Ramadan-themed decorations and greeting cards, fostering their understanding of the significance of Ramadan in a fun and interactive way.

Encouraging Children's Participation in Taraweeh Prayers

Taraweeh prayers hold great importance during Ramadan, and children are encouraged to actively participate in these nightly prayers. Mosques often provide separate prayer areas for children, allowing them to join their peers and learn the rituals of prayer. This enables children to experience the spiritual ambiance of Ramadan and develop a sense of community and devotion.

Cultivating Charity and Generosity

Charitable acts are deeply ingrained in the fabric of Ramadan, and children play an active role in these acts of kindness. Parents encourage their children to donate toys, clothes, and food to those in need. Children also participate in fundraising events organized by schools and community centers, collecting money for charitable organizations. These activities instill in children the values of compassion, generosity, and empathy towards others.

Nurturing Creativity with Ramadan Crafts and Decorations

Children in Iraq enthusiastically participate in creating Ramadan crafts and decorations. They craft vibrant lanterns, known as "fanoos," using paper and string. These lanterns are then hung around the house and in the streets, creating a festive atmosphere .Additionally, children create paper crescent moons and stars, which they use to adorn their rooms and windows. These creative endeavors not only enhance the visual appeal of Ramadan but also allow children to express their artistic abilities and experience a sense of accomplishment.

Embracing Traditional Games and Activities

During Ramadan, children in Iraq engage in various traditional games and activities that bring joy and foster a sense of community. One popular game is "Musaharati," where a person walks through the streets before dawn, banging a drum to wake people up for the pre-dawn meal. Children often join in the Musaharati tradition, adding to the excitement and creating a lively atmosphere in the neighborhood. Another cherished activity is "Gergaoun," where children dress up in traditional attire and go door-to-door, singing songs and receiving sweets and treats from their neighbors. These games and activities not only create lasting memories but also strengthen the bonds among children during Ramadan.

Cherishing Ramadan Iftar for Children

Iftar, the meal to break the fast, holds a special significance for families in Iraq. Children eagerly await the call to prayer, signaling the end of the fast, and gather around the table with their parents and siblings. Special dishes and sweets are prepared specifically for children, such as "kleicha" (date-filled cookies) and "qatayef" (sweet stuffed pancakes). This time of togetherness and feasting creates cherished memories for children and strengthens family bonds.

Engaging in Night of Power (Laylat al-Qadr) Activities

On the Night of Power, children in Iraq actively participate in various activities to commemorate this significant night. They join their families in visiting the mosque for special prayers and recitation of the Quran. Children also engage in acts of worship, such as reciting supplications and seeking forgiveness. Parents often share stories and teachings about the importance of this night, instilling a sense of reverence and spirituality in their children.

In conclusion, Ramadan customs for children in Iraq revolve around instilling the values of fasting, engaging in special activities, and involving them in acts of charity and worship. These customs not only foster a sense of belonging and identity but also help children develop a strong moral compass and a deep understanding of their faith.

NIGHT OF POWER (LAYLAT AL-QADR)

SIGNIFICANCE OF LAYLAT AL-QADR

Laylat al-Qadr, also known as the Night of Power, holds a profound significance in the Islamic calendar. It is believed to be the night when the first verses of the Quran were revealed to Prophet Muhammad (peace be upon him) by Allah. While the exact date of Laylat al-Qadr remains unknown, it is commonly observed during the last ten nights of Ramadan, with the odd nights being particularly revered.

The Night of Power in Islamic Belief

Within Islamic belief, Laylat al-Qadr is regarded as a night of immense blessings and divine mercy. It is believed that during this sacred night, the gates of heaven are opened, and angels descend to the earthly realm. The atmosphere is filled with serenity and tranquility, and the prayers and supplications offered during this time are believed to hold a higher likelihood of being answered by Allah.

The significance of Laylat al-Qadr is emphasized in the Quran, specifically in Surah Al-Qadr (Chapter 97). This chapter describes the night as being more valuable than a thousand months, underscoring its immense worth and importance in the eyes of Allah.

Worship and Prayers on Laylat al-Qadr

Muslims worldwide eagerly anticipate the arrival of Laylat al-Qadr and engage in various acts of worship and devotion throughout this blessed night. It is a time dedicated to prayer, recitation of the Quran, and supplication to Allah. Many Muslims strive to remain awake throughout the night, seeking the blessings and rewards associated with this special occasion.

One of the most common practices on Laylat al-Qadr is the performance of Taraweeh prayers, special night prayers conducted in congregation at the mosque. These prayers consist of additional units of prayer and are often completed over the course of the entire month of Ramadan, with the final portion recited on Laylat al-Qadr.

Mosque Activities on Laylat al-Qadr

Mosques play a central role in the observance of Laylat al-Qadr. They become gathering places for worshippers who come together to engage in acts of devotion and seek the blessings of this auspicious night. Mosques are adorned with beautiful decorations, and special arrangements are made to accommodate the increased number of attendees.

Mosque activities on Laylat al-Qadr include the recitation of the Quran, group prayers, and religious lectures. Imams and scholars deliver sermons that focus on the significance of the night and provide guidance on how to make the most of this blessed occasion. Many mosques also organize community iftars (the breaking of the fast) and suhoor (pre-dawn meal) gatherings to foster a sense of unity and spirituality among worshippers.

Traditions and Customs on Laylat al-Qadr

In addition to the religious practices, Laylat al-Qadr in Iraq is accompanied by various traditions and customs. Families come together to observe this special night, engaging in acts of worship collectively. They spend the night in prayer, recitation of the Quran, and supplication, seeking forgiveness and blessings from Allah.

A common tradition is the preparation of special meals that are shared with neighbors, friends, and the less fortunate. This act of charity and generosity is believed to bring blessings and rewards during Laylat al-Qadr. Additionally, many families engage in acts of charity by donating to the poor and needy, ensuring that everyone can partake in the joy and blessings of this sacred night.

Another cherished tradition on Laylat al-Qadr is the illumination of mosques and homes with lanterns and candles. The soft glow of these lights symbolizes the spiritual enlightenment and guidance sought during this night. Streets and neighborhoods are adorned with lights, creating a serene and peaceful atmosphere.

In conclusion, Laylat al-Qadr holds immense significance in the hearts and minds of Muslims in Iraq. It is a night of intense worship, reflection, and supplication. The traditions and customs associated with this night bring families and communities together, fostering a sense of unity and spirituality. Muslims eagerly await the arrival of Laylat al-Qadr, seeking the blessings and mercy of Allah, and striving to make the most of this special night.

WORSHIP AND PRAYERS ON LAYLAT AL-QADR

Laylat al-Qadr, also known as the Night of Power, holds a profound significance during the holy month of Ramadan in Iraq. It is believed to be the night when the first verses of the Quran were revealed to Prophet Muhammad (peace be upon him). This sacred night is highly revered and considered more valuable than a thousand months of worship. Let's explore the various aspects of worship and prayers observed on Laylat al-Qadr in Iraq.

The Significance of Laylat al-Qadr

Laylat al-Qadr is a night of immense blessings and forgiveness. It is believed that on this night, the gates of heaven are opened, and prayers are readily accepted. Muslims in Iraq eagerly seek the blessings of this night by engaging in various acts of worship and devotion. Although the exact date of Laylat al-Qadr is uncertain, it is commonly observed during the last ten nights of Ramadan, particularly on the odd-numbered nights.

Night Prayers (Qiyam al-Layl)

One of the most prevalent practices on Laylat al-Qadr is performing night prayers, also known as Qiyam al-Layl or Taraweeh prayers. Muslims gather in mosques or homes to participate in prolonged prayers, recitation of the Quran, and supplication. These prayers are conducted after the Isha prayer and can extend for several hours. The recitation of the Quran during these prayers is done with deep reflection and contemplation, aiming for spiritual enlightenment and a closer connection with Allah.

Recitation of the Quran

The recitation of the Quran holds special significance on Laylat al-Qadr. Muslims in Iraq strive to recite as much of the Quran as possible, seeking the blessings and rewards associated with this auspicious night. Many individuals engage in individual recitation, while others participate in group recitation sessions in mosques or homes. The recitation is performed with utmost devotion and concentration, as Muslims believe that the rewards for reciting the Quran on this night are multiplied.

Supplication and Dua

Laylat al-Qadr is a night of intense supplication and dua (prayer). Muslims in Iraq spend the night in deep prayer, seeking forgiveness, guidance, and blessings from Allah. They engage in personal conversations with Allah, pouring out their hearts and seeking His mercy and compassion. The atmosphere is filled with a profound sense of humility and devotion as individuals reflect on their actions and seek repentance.

Itikaf

Some Muslims in Iraq observe Itikaf during the last ten days of Ramadan, including Laylat al-Qadr. Itikaf involves secluding oneself in a mosque or a designated area for a specific period, dedicating the time solely to worship and reflection. This practice allows individuals to detach from worldly distractions and focus entirely on their spiritual connection with Allah. Many individuals choose to observe Itikaf during the last ten nights of Ramadan, hoping to capture the blessings of Laylat al-Qadr.

Acts of Charity and Good Deeds

Laylat al-Qadr is a night of immense blessings, and Muslims in Iraq strive to maximize their good deeds and acts of charity on this night. They engage in various charitable acts, such as feeding the poor, donating to charitable organizations, and helping those in need. The belief is that any act of kindness and charity performed on this night carries multiplied rewards. Muslims also make a conscious effort to be kind, forgiving, and compassionate towards others, seeking to embody the teachings of Islam.

Seeking Forgiveness and Repentance

Laylat al-Qadr is a night of seeking forgiveness and repentance. Muslims in Iraq take the opportunity to reflect on their actions and seek forgiveness from Allah for any wrongdoings or sins committed. They engage in sincere repentance, vowing to rectify their behavior and seek a closer relationship with Allah.

The night is seen as an opportunity for spiritual renewal and purification, allowing individuals to start afresh and seek Allah's mercy and forgiveness.

Personal Reflection and Contemplation

Laylat al-Qadr provides a unique opportunity for personal reflection and contemplation. Muslims in Iraq take the time to reflect on their spiritual journey, their relationship with Allah, and their purpose in life. They contemplate the teachings of Islam and how they can apply them to their daily lives. The night encourages individuals to introspect and make positive changes in their behavior, seeking to become better Muslims and better human beings.

In conclusion, Laylat al-Qadr holds a profound spiritual significance for Muslims in Iraq during the holy month of Ramadan. It is a night of worship, prayers, recitation of the Quran, supplication, acts of charity, seeking forgiveness, and personal reflection. Muslims in Iraq embrace the blessings and opportunities of Laylat al-Qadr to strengthen their faith and deepen their connection with Allah. This sacred night serves as a reminder of the importance of devotion, self-reflection, and acts of kindness in the lives of believers. By engaging in these practices, Iraqi Muslims strive to embody the teachings of Islam and seek spiritual growth during the blessed month of Ramadan.

MOSQUE ACTIVITIES ON LAYLAT AL-QADR

Laylat al-Qadr, known as the Night of Power, holds great

importance during the holy month of Ramadan, particularly for Muslims in Iraq. It is believed to be the night when the first verses of the Quran were revealed to Prophet Muhammad (peace be upon him). Mosques in Iraq play a central role in facilitating worship and fostering a sense of community on this special night.

Night Prayers (Qiyam-ul-Layl)

Mosques become centers of spiritual devotion on Laylat al-Qadr, as worshippers gather to perform night prayers, also known as Qiyam-ul-Layl or Taraweeh prayers. These voluntary prayers are conducted after the Isha prayer and involve reciting portions of the Quran in congregation. The recitation is often extended, with the aim of completing the entire Quran by the end of Ramadan. Many mosques in Iraq organize special programs for Qiyam-ul-Layl, inviting renowned reciters and scholars to lead the prayers and deliver inspiring sermons.

Recitation and Reflection

Mosques provide a serene environment for individuals to engage in the recitation of the Quran and reflect upon its teachings. On Laylat al-Qadr, mosques are filled with worshippers who spend the night reciting verses from the Quran and contemplating their meanings. This act of devotion is believed to bring immense blessings and spiritual enlightenment. In Iraq, mosques often organize Quran recitation competitions, encouraging community members, especially children, to participate and showcase their memorization skills.

Special Lectures and Sermons

Mosques invite knowledgeable scholars and speakers to deliver special lectures and sermons on Laylat al-Qadr. These sessions focus on the significance of the night, its historical context, and the importance of seeking forgiveness and engaging in acts of worship. The aim is to inspire and motivate individuals to make the most of this blessed night and deepen their connection with Allah. Community members eagerly attend these lectures, seeking guidance and spiritual nourishment.

Dua (Supplication) and Seeking Forgiveness

Laylat al-Qadr is a night of intense supplication and seeking forgiveness from Allah. Mosques provide a conducive environment for individuals to engage in dua and seek repentance for their sins. Many mosques organize collective dua sessions, where worshippers gather together and recite specific supplications recommended for this night. The atmosphere is filled with humility and devotion as individuals pour out their hearts, seeking mercy and blessings from the Almighty.

Itikaf (Seclusion in the Mosque)

A spiritual practice known as Itikaf is observed by many devout Muslims in Iraq during the last ten nights of Ramadan, including Laylat al-Qadr. Itikaf involves secluding oneself in the mosque for a specific period, dedicating time solely to worship and reflection. Mosques provide designated areas for individuals to stay and engage in acts of worship, such as recitation of the Quran, dua, and reflection. Itikaf allows individuals to detach from worldly distractions and focus solely on their spiritual connection with Allah.

Community Iftar and Suhoor

Mosques often organize community iftar and suhoor meals on Laylat al-Qadr. These meals provide an opportunity for community members to break their fast together and share in the blessings of the night. Generous individuals or organizations within the community sponsor the meals, providing food and drinks for everyone present. The atmosphere is one of unity and camaraderie as people come together to strengthen their bonds and partake in the blessings of Ramadan.

Night Vigils and Remembrance of Allah

Throughout the night of Laylat al-Qadr, mosques remain open for worshippers to engage in night vigils and remembrance of Allah. Many individuals spend the night in the mosque, engaging in acts of worship such as recitation of the Quran, dua, and dhikr (remembrance of Allah). The atmosphere is filled with tranquility and devotion as worshippers strive to make the most of this auspicious night. The mosque becomes a sanctuary for spiritual rejuvenation and a place where individuals can seek closeness to Allah.

In conclusion, mosques in Iraq play a vital role in facilitating various activities on Laylat al-Qadr. These activities include night prayers, Quran recitation, special lectures, supplication, Itikaf, community meals, and night vigils. The mosque serves as a spiritual hub, bringing the community together and providing a space for individuals to engage in acts of worship and reflection. Laylat al-Qadr holds immense significance for Muslims in Iraq, and the mosque activities on this night contribute to the overall spiritual experience of Ramadan.

TRADITION AND CUSTOMS ON LAYLAT AL-QADR

Laylat al-Qadr, known as the Night of Power, holds immense spiritual significance during the holy month of Ramadan in Iraq. This section explores the unique traditions and customs observed by Iraqi Muslims on this special night.

Embracing the Night of Power

Iraqi Muslims eagerly await the arrival of Laylat al-Qadr and engage in various activities to embrace its blessings. Many devotees spend the entire night in prayer and supplication, seeking forgiveness and divine blessings. They believe that the rewards of worship on this night are multiplied manifold, motivating them to make the most of this auspicious occasion.

Night Prayers and Quran Recitation

Mosques in Iraq come alive on Laylat al-Qadr as worshippers gather to perform special night prayers known as Taraweeh. These congregational prayers consist of additional units of prayer, accompanied by the recitation of the Quran. The aim is to complete the entire Quran by the end of Ramadan, emphasizing the importance of the Quranic teachings on this blessed night.

Reflection and Spiritual Growth

Laylat al-Qadr serves as a time for deep reflection and spiritual growth for many Iraqis. It is an opportunity to introspect, seek forgiveness for past mistakes, and make resolutions for self-improvement. Individuals engage in personal contemplation, aiming for spiritual renewal and a fresh start. The night becomes a catalyst for positive change and a deeper connection with one's faith.

Acts of Charity and Generosity

Charitable acts hold great significance during Ramadan, and Laylat al-Qadr is no exception. Iraqis embrace the spirit of giving by generously donating to the less fortunate, providing food to the needy, and supporting charitable organizations. The night becomes a reminder to extend a helping hand and show compassion to those in need, embodying the values of Islam.

Supplications and Prayers

Iraqi Muslims engage in fervent supplications and prayers on Laylat al-Qadr. They recite specific prayers, seeking blessings for themselves, their families, and the entire Muslim community. Many devotees spend the night reciting the 99 names of Allah, seeking His mercy and forgiveness. The atmosphere is filled with devotion and a profound sense of spiritual connection.

Observing Itikaf

During Laylat al-Qadr, many devout Iraqis choose to observe Itikaf, a spiritual retreat that involves seclusion in the mosque for a specific period, typically during the last ten days of Ramadan. By disconnecting from worldly distractions and immersing themselves in worship, they seek closeness to Allah and focus solely on spiritual matters. Itikaf becomes a time of introspection, self-reflection, and seeking divine guidance.

Sharing Special Nighttime Meals

In Iraq, families come together on Laylat al-Qadr to prepare and share special meals with loved ones. These meals often feature traditional Iraqi dishes, such as biryani, kebabs, and delectable sweets. Breaking the fast and enjoying the blessings of the night becomes a joyous occasion filled with gratitude. The atmosphere is infused with love, togetherness, and appreciation for the opportunity to partake in this blessed night.

Engaging in Night Vigil

Many Iraqis choose to stay awake throughout the night, engaging in acts of worship and remembrance of Allah. They recite the Quran, engage in dhikr (remembrance of Allah), and perform additional voluntary prayers. The night is seen as a time of heightened spirituality, and staying awake is believed to bring immense blessings and rewards. The peacefulness of the night allows for a deeper connection with the divine.

Seeking Forgiveness and Mercy

Laylat al-Qadr is regarded as a night of forgiveness and mercy.

Iraqi Muslims seize this opportunity to seek forgiveness for their sins and ask for Allah's mercy. They engage in heartfelt repentance, acknowledging their mistakes, and seeking redemption. The night becomes a chance to cleanse the soul and seek Allah's forgiveness with utmost sincerity and humility.

In conclusion, Laylat al-Qadr holds great significance in the hearts and minds of Iraqi Muslims. It is a night of intense worship, reflection, and seeking divine blessings. Iraqis embrace various traditions and customs to fully embrace the essence of this special night, including prayers, Quran recitation, acts of charity, and seeking forgiveness. Laylat al-Qadr serves as a reminder of the importance of spirituality and personal growth during the holy month of Ramadan.

EID AL-FITR

PREPARATION FOR EID AL-FITR: CREATING A FESTIVE ATMOSPHERE

Eid al-Fitr, known as the Festival of Breaking the Fast, is a joyous celebration that marks the end of Ramadan in Iraq. The preparations for this special occasion begin well in advance, as families and communities come together to make it a truly memorable and festive time.

Sprucing Up the Home

One of the initial steps in preparing for Eid al-Fitr is sprucing up the home. Iraqi families take great pride in ensuring that their houses are spotless and beautifully decorated for this festive occasion. Every nook and cranny is thoroughly cleaned, creating a fresh and welcoming environment for the celebrations.

In addition to cleaning, families adorn their homes with colorful lights, lanterns, and traditional ornaments. These decorations add a touch of festivity and create an atmosphere of joy and excitement. Many families also hang up special Eid banners and signs, spreading messages of happiness and unity.

Finding the Perfect Outfits

Another important aspect of preparing for Eid al-Fitr in Iraq is finding the perfect outfits. It is customary for both children and adults to wear new clothes on this special day. Iraqi markets and shopping centers buzz with activity as families search for the ideal attire to wear for the Eid prayers and gatherings.

While traditional Iraqi clothing, such as the dishdasha for men and the abaya for women, is often preferred, modern and fashionable styles are also popular, especially among the younger generation. The vibrant colors and intricate designs of the clothes reflect the festive spirit of Eid al-Fitr.

Delightful Sweets and Treats

No celebration in Iraq is complete without delicious food, and Eid al-Fitr is no exception. Iraqi families indulge in baking a variety of traditional sweets and treats to share with loved ones and guests during the festivities. Popular delicacies include kleicha, a date-filled pastry, and baklava, a sweet pastry made with layers of filo dough and nuts.

The process of baking these delectable treats often begins a few days before Eid al-Fitr. Families gather in the kitchen, working together to prepare the dough, fillings, and toppings. The aroma of freshly baked sweets fills the air, creating a sense of anticipation and excitement for the upcoming celebrations.

Exchanging Tokens of Love

Just like in many other cultures, exchanging gifts is an integral part of Eid al-Fitr celebrations in Iraq. Families and friends exchange presents as a gesture of love, appreciation, and goodwill. The gifts can range from small tokens of affection to more elaborate and thoughtful presents.

In addition to buying gifts for family and friends, parents often take delight in purchasing toys and treats for their children. It is a tradition to surprise the little ones with new toys, clothes, and sweets on the morning of Eid al-Fitr. This brings immense joy to the children and adds to the overall excitement and happiness of the day.

Strengthening Bonds through Visits

Eid al-Fitr is a time for strengthening bonds and fostering community spirit. In Iraq, it is customary for families to visit their relatives, friends, and neighbors during this festive period. These visits provide an opportunity to exchange greetings, share meals, and spend quality time together.

Iraqi households warmly welcome their guests, offering them traditional sweets, snacks, and refreshing drinks. The atmosphere is filled with laughter, conversations, and the joy of reconnecting with loved ones. These visits not only strengthen family ties but also promote a sense of unity and solidarity within the community.

Extending a Helping Hand

Charitable acts hold great significance during Eid al-Fitr in Iraq. It is a time when people express their gratitude for the blessings they have received by helping those in need. Many families donate money, food, and clothes to charitable organizations or directly to individuals who are less fortunate.

Zakat al-Fitr, a form of obligatory charity, is also given before the Eid prayers. This donation is meant to purify the fast and provide assistance to those who are unable to celebrate Eid al-Fitr with abundance. The act of giving during this time reinforces the values of compassion, empathy, and generosity within Iraqi society.

In conclusion, the preparations for Eid al-Fitr in Iraq involve sprucing up the home, finding the perfect outfits, indulging in delightful sweets and treats, exchanging tokens of love, strengthening bonds through visits, and extending a helping hand to those in need. These preparations create an atmosphere of joy, unity, and gratitude, making Eid al-Fitr a truly memorable and cherished occasion for the Iraqi people.

EID PRAYERS AND SERMONS: A CELEBRATION OF UNITY AND GRATITUDE

Eid al-Fitr, known as the Festival of Breaking the Fast, is a joyous occasion that marks the end of Ramadan. It is a time of celebration and gratitude for Muslims worldwide, including in Iraq. The day commences with special prayers and sermons that hold a significant place in the heart of the Eid festivities.

The Significance of Eid Prayers

Eid prayers hold immense importance in the Islamic faith and are considered obligatory for all adult Muslims. These prayers are performed collectively, led by an imam. In Iraq, the prayers are usually held in spacious open areas, such as parks or designated prayer grounds, to accommodate the large number of worshipers.

The prayers serve as a means for Muslims to express their gratitude to Allah for the strength and perseverance demonstrated throughout the month of Ramadan. Additionally, they provide an opportunity for the community to come together, strengthening the bonds of brotherhood and sisterhood.

The Sermons: Inspiring Reflection and Unity

Following the Eid prayers, the imam delivers a sermon, also known as a khutbah, which plays a vital role in the Eid celebration. The sermon typically focuses on themes of gratitude, unity, and reflection. It serves as a reminder for Muslims to continue practicing the values and lessons learned during Ramadan throughout the year.

The imam may also address current issues affecting the Muslim community, offering guidance on navigating challenges while upholding Islamic principles. The sermons aim to inspire and motivate worshipers to lead righteous lives and make positive contributions to society.

The Rituals of Eid Prayers: A Sacred Communal Experience

The rituals of Eid prayers follow a specific format. Before the prayers, Muslims are encouraged to perform ablution (wudu) to purify themselves. They dress in their finest attire, often donning traditional clothing, as a sign of respect and honor for the occasion.

The prayers consist of two units (rak'ahs) and are performed collectively. The imam leads the prayer, and the worshippers follow his movements, including standing, bowing, and prostrating. The prayers are recited in Arabic, the language of the Quran, and include specific supplications and verses from the holy book. After the prayers, it is customary for Muslims to exchange greetings of "Eid Mubarak" (Blessed Eid) and embrace one another, symbolizing love and unity. This gesture embodies the spirit of forgiveness and reconciliation emphasized during Eid.

The Role of the Imam: Guiding the Community

The imam plays a crucial role in leading the Eid prayers and delivering the sermon. They are respected figures within the community, chosen for their knowledge of Islamic teachings and their ability to inspire and guide others.

The imam's sermon is an opportunity for them to address the community and provide spiritual guidance. They may discuss the importance of upholding the values and principles of Islam, fostering unity, and promoting social justice. The imam's words carry weight and are meant to encourage worshippers to lead righteous lives and contribute positively to society.

Women and Eid Prayers: Inclusion and Connection

In Iraq, women are encouraged to attend the Eid prayers, although it is not obligatory for them. Many women choose to participate in the prayers, while others may prefer to pray at home. In some areas, separate prayer areas or sections are designated for women to ensure their comfort and privacy.

The inclusion of women in the Eid prayers reflects the inclusive nature of Islam and the importance of their presence in communal worship. It also provides an opportunity for women to connect with other members of the community and strengthen their bonds.

The Spirit of Eid: A Time for Joy and Generosity

Eid prayers and sermons are not merely religious rituals; they are a celebration of faith, unity, and gratitude. The prayers bring the community together, fostering a sense of belonging and camaraderie. The sermons serve as a reminder of the values and principles that Muslims strive to uphold.

Eid is a time of joy and celebration, and the prayers and sermons set the tone for the festivities that follow. It is a time for families and friends to come together, exchange gifts, share meals, and engage in acts of charity. The spirit of Eid is one of love, compassion, and generosity, and the prayers and sermons help reinforce these values.

In conclusion, Eid prayers and sermons hold a special place in the Eid al-Fitr celebrations in Iraq. They provide an opportunity for Muslims to express gratitude, seek spiritual guidance, and strengthen their bond as a community. The prayers and sermons serve as a reminder of the values and principles of Islam, inspiring worshippers to lead righteous lives and contribute positively to society. Eid prayers and sermons set the stage for the joyous festivities that follow, where families and friends come together to celebrate, exchange gifts, and engage in acts of kindness. The spirit of Eid is one of unity, compassion, and generosity, and the prayers and sermons help nurture and reinforce these values within the community. As the day of Eid unfolds, the prayers and sermons serve as a reminder of the blessings of Ramadan and the continuous journey of faith for Muslims in Iraq and beyond.

EID TRADITION AND CUSTOMS

Eid al-Fitr, known as the "Festival of Breaking the Fast," is a joyous celebration that marks the end of Ramadan. In Iraq, this festival is embraced with great enthusiasm, bringing families and communities together. The customs and traditions associated with Eid al-Fitr in Iraq are deeply rooted in the country's cultural heritage and Islamic practices. Let's explore the unique customs and traditions observed during this festive occasion.

Preparations for Eid al-Fitr

In the days leading up to Eid al-Fitr, Iraqis engage in various preparations to ensure a memorable celebration. A significant aspect of these preparations is the thorough cleaning of homes. Families meticulously clean their houses, ensuring a fresh and welcoming environment for their guests. Additionally, they adorn their homes with vibrant lights, lanterns, and traditional ornaments, creating a festive ambiance.

Another important aspect of the preparations is shopping for new clothes. It is customary for Iraqis to purchase new attire for themselves and their children to wear on the day of Eid. The markets and shopping centers bustle with excitement as people search for the perfect outfits. Traditional Iraqi clothing, such as the dishdasha for men and the abaya for women, is often favored for this special occasion.

Eid Prayers and Sermons

On the morning of Eid al-Fitr, Iraqis rise early to attend the special Eid prayers at local mosques. Men, women, and children dress in their finest garments and gather in large congregations to perform the prayers. The prayers are led by the imam, who delivers a sermon emphasizing the values of gratitude, forgiveness, and unity within the Muslim community.

Following the prayers, people exchange warm greetings of "Eid Mubarak" and embrace each other as a symbol of love and unity. It is customary for Iraqis to visit the graves of their loved ones during this time, paying their respects and offering prayers for the departed souls.

Traditional Eid Foods

Food holds a central role in the celebrations of Eid al-Fitr in Iraq. Families prepare a variety of traditional dishes and sweets to share with loved ones and guests. One of the most beloved dishes is "Qeema," a flavorful minced meat dish cooked with aromatic spices and served with rice or bread. Other traditional dishes include "Dolma" (stuffed vegetables), "Biryani"

Traditional Eid Foods

Food plays a central role in the celebrations of Eid al-Fitr in Iraq. Families prepare a variety of traditional dishes and sweets to share with their loved ones and guests. One of the most cherished dishes is "Qeema," a flavorful minced meat dish cooked with aromatic spices and served with fragrant rice or bread. Other traditional dishes include "Dolma" (stuffed vegetables), "Biryani" (a fragrant rice dish with meat), and "Kubba" (a savory meat-filled dumpling).

Sweets and desserts are also an essential part of the Eid feast. "Kleicha," a date-filled pastry, holds a special place during this festive occasion. The delicate layers of "Baklava," a sweet pastry made with filo dough and nuts, are also a favorite among Iraqis. Families often exchange trays of sweets and desserts with their neighbors and friends as a gesture of goodwill and celebration.

Celebrations and Festivities

Eid al-Fitr is a time of joy and celebration, and Iraqis engage in various festivities to mark the occasion. One popular tradition is the exchange of gifts among family members and friends. Children, in particular, eagerly anticipate this tradition as they receive new clothes, toys, and sweets from their elders.

Another common custom is the giving of "Eidiyah," a monetary gift given to children by their parents, relatives, and neighbors. This tradition symbolizes blessings and good wishes for the younger generation. Iraqis also enjoy outdoor activities during Eid al-Fitr. Parks and recreational areas are filled with families enjoying picnics, rides, and games. It is a time for people to relax, have fun, and create lasting memories with their loved ones.

Acts of Charity

Acts of charity hold great significance during Eid al-Fitr in Iraq. It is a time when people reach out to the less fortunate and share their blessings. Many individuals and organizations organize food drives and distribute meals to those in need. Donating clothes, money, and other essential items to orphanages and charitable organizations is also a common practice.

Additionally, it is customary for families to invite the poor and needy to their homes for the Eid feast. This act of hospitality and generosity is deeply rooted in Islamic teachings and serves as a reminder of the importance of compassion and empathy towards others.

In conclusion, Eid al-Fitr in Iraq is a time of joy, togetherness, and gratitude. The customs and traditions associated with this festive occasion reflect the rich cultural heritage and Islamic values of the Iraqi people. From the meticulous preparations and heartfelt prayers to the delectable feasts and acts of charity, Eid al-Fitr brings communities closer and strengthens the bonds of love and unity.

As Iraqis clean their homes and decorate them with colorful lights and ornaments, they create a warm and inviting atmosphere for their guests. The tradition of shopping for new clothes adds an element of excitement and anticipation, as families select their finest attire to wear on this special day.

The morning of Eid al-Fitr is marked by congregational prayers at local mosques, where the community gathers to seek blessings and express gratitude. The sermons delivered by the imams emphasize the values of unity, forgiveness, and gratitude, reminding everyone of the importance of these virtues in their lives.

Food holds a significant place in the celebrations, with families preparing a variety of traditional dishes and sweets. From the flavorful Qeema to the delicate Kleicha pastries, each dish is prepared with love and care. The exchange of gifts, especially among children, adds an element of joy and excitement to the festivities.

Eid al-Fitr is not only a time for personal celebrations but also a time for acts of charity and giving. Iraqis extend their generosity to those in need, organizing food drives, donating clothes, and inviting the less fortunate to share in the joyous feasts. This spirit of compassion and empathy reflects the true essence of Islam and strengthens the bonds of the community.

In parks and recreational areas, families come together to enjoy outdoor activities, creating cherished memories and strengthening family ties. The laughter of children, the aroma of delicious food, and the joyous atmosphere fill the air, creating a sense of unity and happiness.

Eid al-Fitr in Iraq is a celebration that encompasses the values of gratitude, unity, and compassion. It is a time when families and communities come together to celebrate the end of Ramadan and express their appreciation for the blessings in their lives. Through their customs and traditions, Iraqis showcase their rich cultural heritage and the deep-rooted Islamic values that guide their lives.

CELEBRATION AND FESTIVITIES

Ramadan is a month filled with joy and celebration for Muslims worldwide, and Iraq is no exception. The culmination of Ramadan brings forth the joyous occasion of Eid al-Fitr, a time when families, friends, and communities come together to celebrate. In this section, we will delve into the vibrant celebrations and festivities that grace the landscape of Eid al-Fitr in Iraq.

Preparations for Eid al-Fitr

As Eid al-Fitr approaches, a sense of excitement and anticipation fills the air in Iraq. Families embark on preparations by adorning their homes with cleanliness and purchasing new attire for themselves and their children. Wearing new clothes on the day of Eid symbolizes renewal and a fresh start, adding to the festive spirit.

Eid Prayers and Sermons

On the morning of Eid al-Fitr, Muslims in Iraq gather at mosques or designated prayer grounds to partake in the special Eid prayer. Led by an imam, the prayer is followed by a sermon that serves as a reminder of the importance of gratitude, forgiveness, and unity. The sermon also emphasizes the significance of extending kindness to the less fortunate and spreading joy and happiness during this festive occasion.

Traditional Iraqi Delights

Food takes center stage in the celebrations of Eid al-Fitr in Iraq. Families prepare an array of traditional dishes and delectable sweets to share with loved ones and guests. Among the favorites is "Qeema," a spiced minced meat dish served with rice or bread. Other traditional delicacies include "Dolma" (stuffed vegetables), "Kubba" (meat-filled dumplings), and "Biryani" (a flavorful rice dish). For dessert, Iraqis indulge in sweet treats like "Baklava" (layers of filo pastry filled with nuts and sweet syrup) and "Kleicha" (date-filled cookies).

Visiting Loved Ones

Eid al-Fitr serves as a time for reconnecting with family and friends in Iraq. Following the morning prayers, Iraqis visit their relatives, neighbors, and friends to exchange greetings and well wishes. It is customary to bring small gifts or sweets when visiting, and hosts often prepare a generous spread of food and drinks for their guests. These visits strengthen the bonds of kinship and friendship, fostering a sense of unity and togetherness within the community.

Festive Activities and Entertainment

During Eid al-Fitr, Iraqis engage in various festive activities and entertainment. Parks and public spaces come alive with families enjoying picnics, children playing games, and people socializing. Traditional music and dance performances add to the joyful atmosphere, showcasing the rich cultural heritage of Iraq. Additionally, many cities host carnivals and fairs, offering rides, games, and delectable street food. These activities bring delight and amusement to people of all ages, creating cherished memories.

Acts of Generosity

Charitable acts hold a significant place in the Eid al-Fitr celebrations in Iraq. It is believed that extending help to the less fortunate during this blessed time brings immense blessings and rewards. Individuals and organizations organize food drives, distribute clothes and gifts to orphanages, and provide financial assistance to those in need. This spirit of generosity and compassion reflects the true essence of Ramadan and Eid al-Fitr, fostering a sense of empathy and solidarity within the community.

Traditional Customs and Rituals

In addition to the festive activities, several traditional customs and rituals are observed during Eid al-Fitr in Iraq. One such custom is the exchange of "Eidiyah," a small amount of money given to children by their elders as a token of love and blessings. This tradition brings joy to the younger members of the community and instills in them the value of sharing and giving.

Another customary practice is the gathering at the "Eid Gah," a designated area where people come together to offer their prayers and listen to the sermon. The Eid Gah is often a spacious open ground or a specially designated area within a neighborhood or community. It serves as a focal point for the Eid prayers, fostering a sense of unity and collective worship.

Cultural Performances and Art

Eid al-Fitr also serves as a platform to celebrate Iraqi culture and heritage through various artistic performances. Traditional music, dance, and theater performances showcase the richness of Iraqi traditions. These cultural displays not only entertain but also serve as a reminder of the importance of preserving and promoting Iraqi customs and traditions.

In conclusion, Eid al-Fitr in Iraq is a time of immense joy, celebration, and unity. The preparations, prayers, traditional foods, visits to loved ones, festive activities, acts of generosity, and adherence to customs and rituals all contribute to the vibrant and unique atmosphere during this special occasion. The celebrations and festivities of Eid al-Fitr in Iraq reflect the deep-rooted traditions and values of the Iraqi people, fostering a sense of togetherness, compassion, and gratitude within the community.

As the days of Ramadan come to an end, the anticipation for Eid al-Fitr builds, and the preparations intensify. Families meticulously clean their homes, ensuring a welcoming environment for guests and loved ones. The bustling markets are filled with shoppers, eager to find the perfect outfits for themselves and their children. The vibrant colors and traditional designs of the attire add to the festive ambiance.

REFLECTIONS ON RAMADAN

PERSONAL REFLECTIONS AND INSPIRATIONAL STORIES

Ramadan, a sacred month observed by Muslims worldwide, holds a special place in the hearts of Iraqis. In this section, we delve into personal reflections and share inspiring stories from individuals in Iraq, shedding light on their unique experiences during this holy time.

Embracing Family Traditions

One family in Baghdad graciously shared their cherished Ramadan traditions, passed down through generations. Their day begins with the pre-dawn meal, suhoor, where they gather around the table to enjoy a nourishing spread of traditional Iraqi dishes. From masgouf (grilled fish) to dolma (stuffed vegetables) and samoon (Iraqi bread), each bite is savored, providing sustenance for the day of fasting ahead.

Prayer and recitation of the Quran fill the early morning hours, offering solace and spiritual connection. Acts of charity are also an integral part of their Ramadan journey, as they extend a helping hand to those in need, spreading kindness and compassion.

As the sun sets, the family eagerly awaits the call to prayer, signaling the end of the day's fast. Iftar, the meal that breaks the fast, becomes a joyous occasion. The table is adorned with an array of delectable dishes, including beloved Iraqi favorites like biryani, kubba, and baklava. With gratitude in their hearts, the family relishes each morsel, cherishing the blessings of food and the opportunity to share this sacred meal together.

A Vibrant Community Spirit

In a quaint village in southern Iraq, the spirit of Ramadan permeates every corner. The local mosque becomes a focal point for communal activities during this blessed month. Taraweeh prayers, held every evening, bring the community together, as they unite in prayer and immerse themselves in the recitation of the Quran. The melodious voices of the imams resonate, creating an atmosphere of tranquility and devotion.

The village also embraces the tradition of communal iftar gatherings, where families generously contribute dishes to share with their neighbors. This beautiful custom fosters unity and solidarity, transcending differences and strengthening the bonds of friendship and kinship.

During the last ten nights of Ramadan, the village radiates with excitement as Laylat al-Qadr, the Night of Power, approaches. The mosque is adorned with enchanting decorations, and the night is filled with fervent prayers, supplications, and recitation of the Quran. The community holds a deep belief in the immense blessings and mercy bestowed upon them during this sacred night, and they seize the opportunity to make the most of this spiritual occasion.

Cherished Memories of Ramadan

A young girl from Mosul fondly recalls the anticipation and joy that enveloped her neighborhood as Ramadan approached. Colorful lights adorned the streets, and the aroma of mouthwatering delicacies filled the air, creating an atmosphere of celebration and togetherness.

One cherished tradition she remembers is "Gerga'an," a festive celebration that takes place in the middle of Ramadan. Children dress in traditional attire and go door to door, singing songs and receiving sweets and treats from their neighbors. This tradition not only brings delight to the community but also strengthens the bonds between neighbors, fostering a sense of unity and joy.

The young girl also emphasizes the importance of giving during Ramadan. Her family actively prepares food packages and distributes them to those in need, instilling in her a deep sense of empathy, compassion, and responsibility towards her community.

A Journey of Self-Discovery

Ramadan serves as a time of personal introspection and self-improvement for many individuals in Iraq. One man from

Basra shares his transformative journey during this holy month. Fasting enables him to cultivate self-discipline and gain control over his desires. Through abstaining from food and drink, he develops a profound appreciation for the blessings in his life and develops empathy for those less fortunate.

Forgiveness and reconciliation also hold great significance during Ramadan. The man recounts a heartfelt story of reconciling with a close friend during this auspicious month. They met, apologized, and forgave each other, recognizing the power of unity and forgiveness in the spirit of Ramadan.

These personal reflections and inspirational stories illuminate the diverse and meaningful ways in which Ramadan is celebrated in Iraq. From treasured family traditions to vibrant community gatherings, Ramadan serves as a time of spiritual growth, reflection, and connection with others. It is a month that unites people, strengthens bonds, and nurtures a spirit of compassion and generosity.

LESSONS GAINED FROM RAMADAN

Ramadan, a month of introspection, spiritual growth, and self-control, holds great significance for Muslims in Iraq and around the world. During this holy month, fasting, prayer, and acts of charity are observed. As Ramadan draws to a close, it is essential to reflect on the valuable lessons gained during this period and how they can continue to shape our lives beyond this sacred time.

Cultivating Self-Discipline

One of the most profound lessons learned during Ramadan is the cultivation of self-discipline. The practice of fasting from dawn until sunset requires individuals to exercise control over their desires and abstain from food and drink. This practice instills in us the value of self-restraint and the ability to resist temptation. Through fasting, we learn to prioritize our spiritual needs over our physical cravings, a lesson that can be applied to various aspects of our lives beyond Ramadan. The discipline acquired during this month can aid us in maintaining a healthy lifestyle, managing our time effectively, and achieving our goals.

Nurturing Empathy and Compassion

Ramadan encourages Muslims to engage in acts of charity and display compassion towards others. By experiencing hunger and thirst through fasting, we develop empathy for those who face these challenges on a daily basis. This heightened sense of empathy motivates us to be more compassionate and generous, not only during Ramadan but throughout the year. The lessons of empathy and compassion learned during this month remind us of the importance of assisting those in need and making a positive impact on our communities.

Cultivating Gratitude and Appreciation

Fasting during Ramadan teaches us to appreciate the blessings in our lives. When we abstain from food and drink, we become more aware of the basic necessities that we often take for granted. The simple act of breaking our fast at sunset becomes a moment of gratitude and appreciation for the provision of sustenance. This lesson extends beyond physical nourishment and encourages us to be grateful for the blessings of family, health, and opportunities. Ramadan reminds us to express gratitude to Allah and those around us, fostering a sense of contentment and thankfulness.

Strengthening Family Bonds

Ramadan serves as a time for families to come together, break their fast, and engage in worship. The shared experience of fasting and the special moments of iftar and suhoor create opportunities for strengthening family bonds. During this month, families gather around the table, share meals, and engage in meaningful conversations. The lessons learned during Ramadan emphasize the importance of family and the value of spending quality time together. These lessons can be carried forward beyond Ramadan, encouraging us to prioritize our relationships and create lasting memories with our loved ones.

Deepening Spiritual Reflection and Connection

Ramadan provides a unique opportunity for deep spiritual reflection and connection with Allah. The increased focus on prayer, recitation of the Quran, and engaging in acts of worship allows individuals to strengthen their relationship with their Creator. The lessons learned during this month remind us of the significance of maintaining a strong spiritual connection beyond Ramadan. It encourages us to continue seeking knowledge, engaging in acts of worship, and reflecting on our actions and intentions. The spiritual growth experienced during Ramadan can serve as a foundation for a more fulfilling and purposeful life.

Cultivating Resilience and Perseverance

Fasting for an entire month requires resilience and perseverance. The long hours of fasting, particularly during the summer months, can be physically and mentally challenging. However, the lessons learned during Ramadan teach us the importance of perseverance in the face of difficulties. It reminds us that with determination and faith, we can overcome obstacles and achieve our goals. This lesson of resilience can be applied to various aspects of our lives, whether it be in our personal relationships, education, or professional endeavors.

Fostering Unity and Solidarity

Ramadan brings communities together in a spirit of unity and solidarity. Muslims from diverse backgrounds come together to break their fast, pray, and engage in acts of charity. The lessons learned during this month emphasize the importance of unity and working together for the betterment of society. It reminds us that we are part of a larger community and that our actions have an impact on those around us. Beyond Ramadan, these lessons encourage us to foster unity, respect diversity, and contribute positively to our communities.

In conclusion, Ramadan is a month of profound spiritual growth and self-reflection. The lessons gained during this sacred time have a lasting impact on individuals and communities. From cultivating self-discipline and empathy to nurturing gratitude and unity, Ramadan teaches us valuable lessons that can be applied to various aspects of our lives. As we bid farewell to Ramadan, let us carry these lessons forward and strive to embody the values and teachings of this blessed month throughout the year.

IMPACT OF RAMADAN ON IRAQI SOCIETY

Ramadan holds immense significance in Iraqi society, leaving a lasting impact on various aspects of daily life. This sacred month fosters unity, spirituality, and generosity among the people of Iraq, shaping the social fabric of the country.

Strengthening Bonds within Communities

One of the remarkable effects of Ramadan on Iraqi society is the strengthening of community bonds. During this month, individuals come together to break their fasts and share meals with loved ones, friends, and neighbors. The act of inviting others to join in the iftar meal is a common practice, promoting a sense of togetherness and nurturing a spirit of generosity. This tradition not only strengthens family ties but also builds a sense of community and solidarity among Iraqis.

Cultivating Generosity and Charity

Ramadan serves as a catalyst for heightened generosity and charity in Iraqi society. Muslims are encouraged to extend a helping hand to those in need, and this spirit of giving is particularly evident during this holy month. Many individuals and organizations organize charitable initiatives, such as distributing food and essential supplies to the less fortunate. The act of giving is deeply ingrained in Iraqi culture, and Ramadan amplifies acts of kindness and compassion.

Nurturing Spiritual Growth

Ramadan provides a profound opportunity for spiritual reflection and devotion for Muslims in Iraq. The fasting, prayers, and recitation of the Quran during this month allow individuals to deepen their connection with their faith. The emphasis on self-discipline and self-reflection during Ramadan encourages personal growth and spiritual development. This heightened focus on spirituality has a positive impact on the overall well-being of individuals and contributes to a more harmonious society.

Preserving Cultural Heritage

Ramadan traditions in Iraq are deeply rooted in the country's rich cultural heritage. The observance of these traditions helps preserve and promote Iraqi culture. From the preparation of traditional Iraqi dishes to the recitation of ancient prayers, Ramadan serves as a reminder of the importance of cultural identity and heritage. The passing down of these customs from one generation to another ensures the continuity of Iraqi traditions and strengthens the sense of national pride.

Economic Influence

Ramadan also exerts a significant economic influence on Iraqi society. The month-long fasting period leads to changes in consumer behavior and spending patterns. The demand for certain food items and products increases during this time, stimulating the local economy. Additionally, the increased charitable activities and donations during Ramadan contribute to the redistribution of wealth within society, providing support to those in need and fostering economic stability.

Promoting Education and Awareness

Ramadan serves as a platform for education and awareness in Iraqi society. Mosques and community centers organize lectures, seminars, and workshops to educate people about the significance of Ramadan and its teachings. These educational initiatives help foster a better understanding of Islam and promote tolerance and acceptance among different religious and cultural groups. The increased focus on education and awareness during Ramadan contributes to the intellectual development and cultural enrichment of Iraqi society.

Enhancing Health and Well-being

The practice of fasting during Ramadan has a positive impact on the health and well-being of individuals in Iraqi society. The intermittent fasting pattern followed during this month has been associated with various health benefits, including improved insulin sensitivity, weight management, and detoxification. Additionally, the emphasis on consuming nutritious food and maintaining a balanced diet during suhoor and iftar meals promotes healthier eating habits among Iraqis, leading to overall improved health and well-being.

Fostering Unity and National Identity

Ramadan plays a crucial role in fostering a sense of unity and national identity in Iraq. Regardless of their differences, Iraqis come together to observe this holy month, emphasizing their shared values and beliefs. The collective experience of fasting, praying, and engaging in charitable acts creates a sense of belonging and unity among the diverse population of Iraq. Ramadan serves as a reminder of the common bonds that unite Iraqis and strengthens the national identity of the country.

In conclusion, Ramadan has a profound and multifaceted impact on Iraqi society, influencing various aspects of daily life. From strengthening community bonds to promoting generosity, spirituality, and cultural preservation, this holy month shapes the social fabric of Iraq. The economic, educational, and health-related effects of Ramadan further contribute to the overall well-being and development of Iraqi society. As Iraq continues to evolve, the traditions and values associated with Ramadan will undoubtedly play a significant role in shaping the future of the country.

THE FUTURE OF RAMADAN TRADITIONS IN IRAQ: EMBRACING CHANGES AND PRESERVING HERITAGE

Ramadan, a sacred month of fasting and spiritual devotion, holds deep significance for Muslims in Iraq and across the globe. It is a time of reflection, prayer, acts of charity, and communal gatherings that have been cherished for generations, becoming an integral part of Iraqi culture. However, as society evolves and embraces modernity, the future of Ramadan traditions in Iraq may encounter certain challenges and transformations.

Embracing Change in Lifestyles and Ramadan Practices

The changing lifestyles of the Iraqi population may influence the future of Ramadan traditions. In an era of rapid technological advancements and globalization, people's daily routines and habits have undergone significant transformations. The fast-paced nature of modern life can make it more challenging for individuals to fully engage in the spiritual practices of Ramadan.

Traditionally, Ramadan was a time when families and communities would come together for iftar (the meal to break the fast) and taraweeh prayers. However, with the increasing demands of work and other commitments, finding time for these communal activities has become more difficult. As a result, there may be a shift towards more individualized practices during Ramadan, with people focusing on personal reflection and worship in the comfort of their own homes.

Balancing Traditional Values and Western Influences

The influence of Western culture is another factor that may impact the future of Ramadan traditions in Iraq. As Iraq becomes more connected to the global community, there is a growing exposure to Western customs and practices. While this can bring about positive cultural exchange, it may also lead to a dilution of traditional Ramadan traditions as people adopt new ways of celebrating the holy month.

For instance, the concept of Ramadan tents, popular in some Western countries, may start gaining popularity in Iraq. These tents provide a space for people to gather, socialize, and enjoy special Ramadan meals. While this can foster community bonding, it may divert attention away from the traditional practices of attending mosque prayers and engaging in acts of charity.

Nurturing Cultural Preservation and Generational Shifts

Over time, there is often a natural shift in cultural practices from one generation to the next, which can impact the future of Ramadan traditions in Iraq. Younger generations may have different priorities and interests, potentially leading to a gradual decline in the observance of certain traditions.

However, cultural preservationcontinues to play a vital role in maintaining the essence of Ramadan traditions. Many Iraqi families take pride in passing down their cultural heritage to their children and grandchildren. This includes instilling the importance of fasting, acts of charity, and participation in communal prayers. By nurturing these values in the younger generation, there is hope that the traditions of Ramadan will continue to thrive in Iraq.

Embracing Adaptation and Evolution

While challenges and changes may lie ahead, it is important to recognize that traditions are not static entities. They have the ability to evolve and adapt to the needs and circumstances of the times. This adaptability has allowed Ramadan traditions to endure for centuries.

As Iraq continues to develop and progress, it is likely that

Ramadan traditions will also undergo evolution. This evolution may involve incorporating new practices that align with the changing needs of society while still upholding the core values of Ramadan. For example, technology could be harnessed to create virtual platforms for communal prayers and gatherings, enabling people to connect and engage in worship even when physically apart.

The Power of Education and Awareness

Education and awareness play a pivotal role in shaping the future of Ramadan traditions in Iraq. By educating the younger generation about the significance and beauty of Ramadan, they can develop a deeper appreciation for these traditions and be more inclined to continue practicing them.

Mosques, schools, and community organizations have a crucial role to play in promoting the understanding and observance of Ramadan traditions. Through organizing educational programs, workshops, and cultural events, they can create opportunities for people to learn about the history, rituals, and values associated with Ramadan. This knowledge can foster a sense of pride and connection to these traditions, ensuring their preservation for future generations.

In conclusion, the future of Ramadan traditions in Iraq may encounter challenges due to changing lifestyles, the influence of Western culture, and generational shifts. However, by embracing change, nurturing cultural preservation, adapting traditions, and promoting education and awareness, there is hope that these cherished practices will continue to thrive.

Ramadan is a time of spiritual reflection, community bonding, and acts of kindness, and it is essential to preserve the essence of these traditions while embracing the evolving needs of society. By doing so, Iraq can ensure that the rich heritage of Ramadan continues to be celebrated and cherished for generations to come.

Conclusion

SUMMARY OF FINDINGS

In this section, we will provide a concise summary of the key findings and insights gained from our exploration of Ramadan traditions in Iraq.

Significance of Ramadan in Iraqi Culture

Ramadan holds immense significance in Iraqi culture, serving as a time of spiritual reflection, self-discipline, and community bonding. Fasting during this holy month is considered a religious obligation and a means of purifying the soul. It is a time for strengthening faith and seeking forgiveness from Allah.

Preparations for Ramadan

Preparations for Ramadan in Iraq encompass both physical and spiritual aspects. The announcement of Ramadan marks the beginning of anticipation and excitement. Families engage in pre-Ramadan shopping to stock up on essential food items and ingredients for special Ramadan recipes. Cleaning and decorating the house create a welcoming and festive atmosphere.

Fasting during Ramadan

Fasting is the central pillar of Ramadan, observed with great dedication by Iraqis. Abstaining from food and drink from dawn until sunset is seen as a way to develop self-control, empathy, and gratitude. Suhoor, the pre-dawn meal, and Iftar, the meal to break the fast, hold great significance. Traditional Iraqi foods are prepared for Iftar, and families come together to share the meal. Charitable acts, such as providing food to the less fortunate, are also common during Ramadan.

Family and Community Gatherings

Ramadan is a time for strengthening family bonds and fostering community spirit. Iftar gatherings with family and friends are a common occurrence, where people come together to share a meal and engage in meaningful conversations. Mosques play a central role in community activities during Ramadan, organizing Taraweeh prayers and hosting events that bring people together. Visiting relatives and neighbors is also a cherished tradition during this holy month.

Night of Power (Laylat al-Qadr)

Laylat al-Qadr, known as the Night of Power, is considered the holiest night of the year. It is believed to be the night when the first verses of the Quran were revealed to Prophet Muhammad. Iraqi Muslims engage in intense worship and prayers on this night, seeking blessings and forgiveness. Mosques are filled with worshippers, reciting the Quran and engaging in supplications. Various traditions and customs, such as staying awake all night and performing acts of charity, are observed on Laylat al-Qadr.

Eid al-Fitr

Eid al-Fitr marks the end of Ramadan and is a joyous occasion for Iraqis. Preparations for Eid begin well in advance, with families cleaning their homes and purchasing new clothes. On the day of Eid, Muslims gather for special prayers and sermons at mosques. After the prayers, people visit relatives and friends, exchanging greetings and gifts. Traditional Iraqi dishes are prepared, and feasts are shared with loved ones. Celebrations and festivities continue throughout the day, with music, dancing, and games.

Reflections on Ramadan

Ramadan is a transformative month for many Iraqis, providing an opportunity for personal growth and spiritual reflection. Through fasting, prayer, and acts of charity, individuals gain a deeper understanding of their faith and develop a stronger connection with Allah. The lessons learned during Ramadan, such as self-discipline, empathy, and gratitude, have a lasting impact on individuals and contribute to the overall well-being of Iraqi society.

Future of Ramadan Traditions in Iraq

As Iraq continues to evolve and face various challenges, the traditions of Ramadan remain deeply rooted in the culture and identity of its people. While modernization and globalization may bring changes to certain aspects of Ramadan celebrations, the core values and practices are likely to endure. It is important for future generations to embrace and preserve these traditions, as they play a vital role in fostering unity, spirituality, and social cohesion within Iraqi society.

THE FINAL THOUGHTS

In conclusion, the Ramadan traditions in Iraq are a testament to the rich cultural and religious heritage of the country. The month-long observance of fasting, the emphasis on family and community gatherings, and the spiritual reflections during Laylat al-Qadr all contribute to the unique experience of Ramadan in Iraq. This report has provided a comprehensive overview of the various aspects of Ramadan in Iraq, highlighting the importance of this holy month in shaping the lives and values of the Iraqi people.

Recommendations for Further Research

While this report has covered a wide range of topics related to Ramadan traditions in Iraq, there are still areas that warrant further research. Some potential areas for future exploration include the regional variations in Ramadan practices within Iraq, the impact of modernization on traditional Ramadan customs, and the role of Ramadan in promoting interfaith dialogue and understanding. Conducting in-depth interviews and surveys with individuals from different regions and backgrounds would provide valuable insights into these areas of study. Additionally, exploring the evolving role of technology and social media in shaping Ramadan traditions in Iraq could offer intriguing avenues for further research. Understanding how digital platforms are influencing the way people connect, share traditions, and engage in religious practices during Ramadan would provide a contemporary perspective on the evolving nature of these traditions.

Furthermore, investigating the experiences and perspectives of Iraqi diaspora communities and their efforts to maintain and adapt Ramadan traditions in their new cultural contexts would offer a unique and enriching perspective. By delving deeper into these areas, researchers can contribute to a more comprehensive understanding of the dynamic nature of Ramadan traditions in Iraq and their significance in the lives of individuals and communities.

FINAL REFLECTIONS

As we bring this report on Ramadan traditions in Iraq to a close, it is essential to reflect on the profound significance of this sacred month and its profound impact on Iraqi society. Ramadan holds a special place in the hearts of Iraqis, serving as a time for spiritual introspection, community cohesion, and acts of benevolence. Throughout this report, we have delved into various facets of Ramadan in Iraq, from the preparations leading up to the month, to the fasting rituals, family and community gatherings, the Night of Power (Laylat al-Qadr), and the joyous celebration of Eid al-Fitr.

Safeguarding Cultural Heritage

A key takeaway from this report is the role of Ramadan in safeguarding the rich cultural heritage of Iraqis. Despite the challenges faced by the nation, the traditions and customs associated with Ramadan continue to be cherished and passed down from one generation to the next. The emphasis on familial and communal gatherings, the sharing of meals, and acts of charity all contribute to the preservation of Iraqi culture and values.

Fostering Stronger Community Bonds

Ramadan acts as a unifying force in Iraqi society, bringing people together in a spirit of solidarity and compassion. The communal iftar gatherings, both within families and at mosques, provide an opportunity for individuals to connect, strengthen relationships, and cultivate a sense of belonging. These gatherings not only promote social cohesion but also create a supportive network that extends beyond the month of Ramadan.

Nurturing Spiritual Growth

The month of Ramadan is a time of heightened spirituality for Iraqis. The fasting from dawn until sunset, the recitation of the Quran, and the additional prayers during the night all contribute to a deepening of faith and a sense of spiritual rejuvenation. The emphasis on self-discipline, self-reflection, and self-control during this month allows individuals to develop a stronger connection with their faith and seek personal growth.

Lessons in Empathy and Generosity

Ramadan in Iraq is not solely focused on personal spiritual growth but also on extending kindness and generosity to others. The act of giving, whether through providing food for iftar, donating to charitable organizations, or visiting the less fortunate, imparts valuable lessons in empathy and compassion. These acts of charity not only benefit those in need but also foster a sense of social responsibility and solidarity within the community.

Addressing Challenges and Embracing Opportunities

While Ramadan traditions in Iraq continue to thrive, there are also challenges that need to be acknowledged and addressed. Ongoing conflicts and political instability have impacted the ability of some Iraqis to fully engage in the Ramadan rituals. Additionally, the rapid modernization and globalization have introduced new influences that may potentially dilute traditional practices. It is crucial for Iraqi society to find a balance between embracing change and preserving their cultural heritage.

Recommendations for Future Exploration

To gain a deeper understanding of the impact of Ramadan traditions in Iraq, there are several areas that warrant further research. One area of interest could be the role of women in Ramadan and how their contributions shape the overall experience. Additionally, studying the influence of Ramadan on the younger generation and their perspectives on tradition and modernity would provide valuable insights. Furthermore, investigating the economic impact of Ramadan, particularly in terms of consumer spending and market trends, would be beneficial for researchers and policymakers alike.

In conclusion, Ramadan traditions in Iraq are deeply ingrained in the cultural tapestry of the country. The month-long observance of fasting, prayer, and acts of charity not only strengthens the bonds within the community but also fosters personal growth and spiritual reflection. As Iraq continues to navigate through challenges, it is crucial to preserve and celebrate these traditions, ensuring that the values of compassion, empathy, and unity are upheld. Ramadan in Iraq is not just a religious obligation but a time of renewal, connection, and hope for a brighter future.